GIRLS ONLY

NEW
HOLLAND

ONLY

GIRLS

DRINKS, NIBBLES AND FUN
FOR YOUR GIRLS' EVENT

FIONA PEARCE

CONTENTS

GETTING READY FOR YOUR GIRLS' EVENT

So you're preparing for your girls only event. Whether it's a baby shower, hen's party or elegant high tea, or just a girls' night in with fabulous cocktails, food and gossip, this book covers it all. From recipes for food and drinks to post-party hangover cures, 'Girls Only' is packed with information to help your event run as smoothly as a pair of freshly waxed legs.

When it comes to the menu, planning ahead of time is the key to success. You don't want to be caught in the kitchen unable to spend time with your guests. We've tried to cover it all, from quick meals and hearty food if you're serving alcohol, to simple starters and finger food (easier for your guests to nibble, and easier for you in terms of dishes to wash). Some can be prepared in advance and will keep well in the refrigerator 3–4 hours beforehand.

Drinks should be quick to make and not too potent, as you don't want everyone waking up with a hangover the next day, feeling like they had a lousy night. We have included a range of classic recipes, from Martinis and Cosmpolitans to popular cocktails like Pina Coladas and Mai Tais. And if you want to get the party moving even more, you might want to try some fun shots. Remember, though, you don't want your guests falling off the bus and not enjoying themselves, so be careful with the strong spirits.

This book also supplies topics for discussion that will keep the conversation interesting. You don't want a lull in the night and having a few topics to hand will steer your guests away from talking politics or boring small talk. And if you're going for a more active kind of event, like pole dancing or belly dancing, we have some tips that will help make it a great time for everyone.

We've also considered specific special events such as hen's nights, baby showers, the celebration of a friend's happy divorce, and more.

Whatever your plans, we hope we've given you lots of ideas to make your girls' event special. And don't forget – us girls need to stick together!

HAVE A BALL!

Fiona Pearce

PREPARING YOUR MENU

DRINKS

▼ MARTINIS

MARTINI, PEPPERMINT VODKATINI, MANHATTAN, CAMPARI VODKATINI, ABSOLUTE VODKATINI, CARIBBEAN MARTINI, BLOODY MARTINI, BLUE HAWAII MARTINI, BOMBAY MARTINI, DIRTY MARTINI, CITRUS MARTINI, LONDON MARTINI, RUSSATINI, MEXICANA MARTINI, SWEET AND SPICY MARTINI, MARTINI, PEPPERMINT VODKATINI, MANHATTAN, CAMPARI VODKATINI, ABSOLUTE VODKATINI, CARIBBEAN MARTINI, BLOODY MARTINI, BLUE HAWAII MARTINI, BOMBAY MARTINI, DIRTY MARTINI, CITRUS MARTINI, LONDON MARTINI, RUSSATINI, MEXICANA MARTINI, SWEET AND SPICY MARTINI, MARTINI, PEPPERMINT VODKATINI, MANHATTAN, CAMPARI VODKATINI, ABSOLUTE VODKATINI, CARIBBEAN MARTINI, BLOODY MARTINI, BLUE HAWAII MARTINI, BOMBAY MARTINI, DIRTY MARTINI, CITRUS MARTINI, LONDON MARTINI, RUSSATINI, MEXICANA

MIXING MARTINIS

A martini may be shaken (James Bond style), stirred, strained, straight up or on the rocks – it's up to you.

Some martini recipes advise the use of a cocktail shaker and there are two versions widely used. The Boston shaker is the one bartenders use most. It only has two parts, a stainless-steel metal mixing tumbler and a slightly smaller glass tumbler– it has no internal strainer. If using a Boston shaker you will probably need a Hawthorn strainer (the one with a coiled spring around the rim) on hand, as it is easier to use when straining ice or fruit out of a drink. The rolled spring keeps the ice in the shaker while allowing some fruit pulp and even some shards of ice into the glass.

A Cobbler shaker is the classic cocktail shaker, normally made in three pieces. It consists of a stainless-steel metal tumbler, a snug-fitting lid with a strainer and a small cap that fits over the lid and covers the strainer.

To use, place about half a container of good quality cracked ice into the shaker, then pour in the ingredients, seal the top and shake for about 15 to 20 shakes. Don't do this for too long or too vigorously – you don't want to dilute the drink, you only want to make it as cold and lively as possible.

Other fun tools to assist in your martini-mixing include an eye dropper (not for the eyes, silly!) to ensure just the desired amount of vermouth is infused into your cocktail. Mixers are also available, but you have to wonder if these are really required once the first excellent martini goes down.

Some people prefer a stirred martini with a twist. To make a stirred martini, ensure you have a good mixing glass and a muddling spoon (a spoon with a long, twisted handle).

GARNISHING MARTINIS

The quintessential garnish for the martini is an olive. Sometimes not one, but two, from unripe pale green, through brownish, to jet-black. They can be whole, sliced, diced or stuffed with myriad ingredients. Stuffings include cream cheese, blue cheese, chilli peppers and pimento, but if you have any good stuffing ideas, be adventurous and make your own.

The olives used can be small, medium or large (depending on your hunger). When you are shopping for them, try as many as you can. You will eventually find the one that best suits your taste. Of course, martinis are not only garnished with olives, but also with lemon, lime and orange zest, slices, wedges and quarters. Red, green, yellow and white pickled onions can also be used. Sometimes olive brine is also used as an ingredient in the cocktail; you will find this in our 'Dirty Martini'.

One final point on garnishing: never overdo it. If you can't get your mouth near the rim of the glass you have certainly gone too far. Most world-champion cocktails have just a single slice of fruit, a cherry or a strawberry, on the side of the glass, sometimes with the addition of a swizzle stick and/or straw. In longer drinks, straws are always served for a lady, but never for a man.

MARTINI GLASSES

It's not much fun mixing the world's best martini and then pouring it into a plastic cup – there's no elegance there. We recommend you splurge on at least half a dozen of the best 3 oz (90mL) triangle-shaped martini glasses. Also buy four of the larger 5 oz (150mL) glasses and even a couple 8 oz (250mL) glasses, in case you develop a colossal thirst during the party. Remember, the better the quality of the glass, the better the martini experience.

CHILLING THE GLASS

Martinis should be served very cold. To achieve this, run cold water over the glass, then shake off the excess and place it in the refrigerator or freezer, rim down. This will allow the water to drain out and not freeze in the bottom of the glass.

Peppermint Vodkatini

1½ oz (45mL) vodka
½ oz (15mL) white crème de menthe
Fresh mint sprig

Combine liquid ingredients with cracked ice in a cocktail shaker and shake well. Strain into a chilled 3 oz (90mL) martini glass and garnish with the mint sprig.

Manhattan

1½ oz (45mL) rye whiskey
1½ oz (45mL) sweet vermouth
1 dash angostura bitters
Maraschino cherry

Combine liquid ingredients in a mixing glass with ice and stir well. Strain into a chilled 3 oz (90mL) martini glass and garnish with the cherry.

Campari Vodkatini

1½ oz (45mL) vodka
1½ tsp Campari
Lime twist

Combine liquid ingredients with cracked ice in a cocktail shaker and shake well. Strain into a chilled cocktail glass and garnish with lime twist.

Absolute Vodkatini

1½ oz (45mL) vodka
1½ tsp triple sec
½ oz (15mL) fresh lemon juice
1 dash orange bitters
Cocktail olive

Combine liquid ingredients with cracked ice in a cocktail shaker and shake well. Strain into a chilled 3 oz (90mL) martini glass and garnish with the olive.

Caribbean Martini

Granulated sugar
1½ oz (45mL) light rum
1½ tsp dry vermouth
Lime wedge
Lime twist

Place the sugar in a saucer. Rub the lime wedge around the rim of a chilled martini glass, then dip the glass into the sugar to coat the rim. Combine liquid ingredients with cracked ice in a cocktail shaker and shake well. Strain into a 3 oz (90mL) martini glass and garnish with lime twist.

Bloody Martini

2 oz (60mL) gin
Dash of grenadine cordial
1½ tsp dry vermouth

Combine liquid ingredients with cracked ice in a cocktail shaker and shake well. Strain into a chilled 3 oz (90mL) martini glass.

Blue Hawaii Martini

1½ oz (45mL) gin
1½ tsp blue curacao
Lemon twist

Combine liquid ingredients in a mixing glass with ice cubes and stir well. Strain into a chilled 3 oz (90mL) martini glass and garnish with the lemon twist.

Bombay Martini

3 oz (90mL) gin
Splash of dry vermouth
Blue cheese olive

Combine liquid ingredients in a mixing glass with ice cubes and stir well. Strain into a chilled 3 oz (90mL) martini glass and garnish with the blue cheese olive.

Dirty Martini

1½ oz (45mL) gin
½ oz (15mL) dry vermouth
1½ tsp olive brine
2 stuffed cocktail olives

Combine liquid ingredients with cracked ice in a cocktail shaker and shake well. Rub rim of glass with lemon wedge. Strain liquid into a chilled 3 oz (90mL) martini glass and garnish with two olives.

Citrus Martini

1 oz (30mL) gin
½ oz (15mL) dry vermouth
½ oz (15mL) orange juice
Lemon, lime and orange wedges

Combine liquid ingredients with cracked ice in a cocktail shaker and shake well. Strain into a chilled 3 oz (90mL) martini glass. Garnish with fruit wedges.

London Martini

1½ oz (45mL) gin
½ tsp maraschino liqueur
5 dashes of orange bitters
½ tsp caster sugar
Lemon wedge

Combine liquid ingredients in a mixing glass and stir well. Pour mixture into a cocktail shaker with cracked ice and sugar, then shake well. Strain into a chilled 3 oz (90mL) martini glass and garnish with the lemon wedge.

Mexicana Martini

1½ oz (45mL) gin
½ oz (15mL) tequila
1½ tsp Cointreau
1 tsp fresh lime juice
Lime twist

Combine liquid ingredients with cracked ice in a cocktail shaker and shake well. Strain into a chilled 3 oz (90mL) martini glass and garnish with lime twist.

Sweet and Spicy Martini

1½ oz (45mL) gin
1½ tsp sweet vermouth
1½ tsp orange liqueur
Cinnamon stick

Combine liquid ingredients with cracked ice in a cocktail shaker and shake well. Strain into a chilled 3 oz (90mL) martini glass and garnish with the cinnamon stick.

Appletini

2 oz (60mL) vodka
½ oz (15mL) schnapps
½ oz (15mL) apple cider
Apple slice to garnish

Combine liquid ingredients in a cocktail shaker with cracked ice. Shake well and strain into a chilled 5 oz (140mL) cocktail glass. Garnish with an apple slice.

Chocolatini

2 oz (60mL) vodka
1 oz (30mL) Godiva chocolate liqueur
Cocoa powder
Chocolate flake

Wet rim of a 3 oz (90mL) martini glass and dip into cocoa powder. Combine vodka and chocolate liqueur in a cocktail shaker with ice. Shake well to chill. Then strain into the martini glass. Use a chocolate flake for garnish.

Martini

1½ oz (45mL) gin
2/3 oz (20mL) dry vermouth

Stir over ice and strain. Garnish with lemon twist or olive on toothpick in the glass.
The classic, sophisticated black-tie cocktail. Always stirred, but when shaken is known as a Bradford. An olive garnish retains the gin sting whereas a lemon twist makes the cocktail smoother.

Note: A 'dry martini' has less vermouth.

Sweet Martini

1½ oz (45mL) dry gin
2/3 oz (20mL) Rosso vermouth

Stir over ice and strain. Garnish with red cherry on toothpick in glass.
Sister to the 'dry martini', the sweeter Rosso vermouth overwhelms the gin sting.

'On the rocks' – poured into a standard spirit glass over ice.
'Straight up'   shaken or stirred with ice, strained and served into a 3 oz (90mL) cocktail glass without ice.

PREPARING YOUR COCKTAILS & MIXED DRINKS

FABULOUS CONCOCTIONS

When someone says 'cocktails', we imagine a vast range of alcoholic drinks topped with juices, dairy products, sugar syrups or more alcohol, usually shaken and poured over ice. But there is a wide range of other mixed beverages too, from mulled wines to non-alcoholic mocktails. Explore your options.

Make sure you assemble your mixing equipment properly and steadily familiarise yourself with the skills of mixology. If you're an adventurous type, keep detailed notes on the quantities used so you can adjust and vary your recipes with new twists. If the taste is unappealing, my best advice is that it goes down the drain.

Think seasonal as well. Fresh fruits and juices are dynamic in mixed drinks, and at their best when they're in season.

ESSENTIAL EQUIPMENT FOR A FIRST-TIMER

bottle opener

can opener

cocktail shaker (Boston or Cobbler)

cutting board

measuring spoons and cups

mixing glass

sharp knife

strainer

straws

waiter's friend (corkscrew)

FOR THE MORE PROFESSIONAL COCKTAIL MAKER

cloths for cleaning glasses

coasters

electric blender

free pourers

ice bucket

ice scoop

paper towels or napkins

scooper spoon (long-handled teaspoon)

stick muddler

swizzle sticks

GLASSWARE

Highball glasses are for long, cool, refreshing drinks.

Cocktail glasses (e.g. hurricane glasses, Moscow mug) are for novelty drinks. All cocktail glasses should be kept chilled in a refrigerator or filled with ice while you are preparing the cocktail.

Champagne glasses are for creamy, after-dinner style drinks.

A punch bowl is for large quantities of punch or soft drink, served out into glasses with a ladle.

Spirit glasses and tumblers are for classic mixed drinks.

Short glasses are for short, strong drinks that are drunk in one mouthful (shots).

COCKTAIL LINGO

Shake: Mix your cocktail in a shaker by hand.

Stir: Mix the ingredients by stirring them with ice in a mixing glass and then straining them into a chilled cocktail glass.

Build: Mix the ingredients in the glass in which the cocktail will be served, floating one on top of the other.

Blend: Mix the ingredients using an electric blender or mixer. Tip: add fruit first, then alcohol.

Muddle: Crush fruit or mint in a glass with the muddler end of a bar spoon.

Frosting: Coat the rim of the glass with either salt or sugar.

Garnishing: Decorate the cocktail. Remember, simplicity is everything when garnishing cocktails.

Handling Ice: Ice is a vital ingredient. It must be clean and fresh at all times.

Handling fruit juices: If you are planning to use fruit, ensure it is in season, fresh or in date from a can.

Banana Colada

Glass: 10½ oz (300mL) fancy glass

1 oz (30mL) Bacardi rum
1 oz (30mL) sugar syrup
1 oz (30mL) coconut cream
1 oz (30mL) cream
4 oz (120mL) pineapple juice
½ banana

Build with ice and pour.
Garnish with a slice of banana, pineapple spear and mint leaves. Serve with straws.
Be adventurous and surprise yourself!

Brandy Alexander

Glass: 5 oz (140mL) Champagne saucer

1 oz (30mL) brandy
1 oz (30mL) dark crème de cacao liqueur
1/6 oz (5mL) grenadine cordial
1 oz (30mL) cream

Shake with ice and strain.
Garnish with a sprinkle of nutmeg and a cherry.
Cognac may be substituted for brandy to deliver an
exceptional aftertaste.

Daiquiri

Glass: 5 oz/140mL Champagne saucer

1½ oz (45mL) rum
1 oz (30mL) pure lemon juice
½ oz (15mL) sugar syrup
½ egg white, optional

Shake with ice and strain.
Garnish with a lemon slice or lemon spiral.
Ideal for large parties, as batches can be stored ready for instant use. Mango, when in season, is very popular. When mixing a pure fruit daiquiri, it is best to use an electric blender and blend well with ice, then strain into a Champagne saucer.

Pina Colada

Glass: 9 oz (265mL) highball glass

1 oz (30mL) rum
1 oz (30mL) coconut cream
1 oz (30mL)sugar syrup
4 oz (125mL) unsweetened pineapple juice

Shake with ice and pour.
Garnish with pineapple wedge, three leaves and a cherry, serve with straws and swizzle stick.
This is another tropical Hawaiian cocktail distinguished by the inclusion of coconut cream. If coconut cream is unavailable, coconut liqueur will suffice; the cream is optional for a richer blend.

Toblerone

Glass: 5 oz/140mL cocktail glass

1 tsp Baileys Irish Cream
½ oz (15mL) Kahlúa
½ oz (15mL) white crème de cacao
1 oz (30mL) Frangelico
2 oz (60mL) cream
½ tsp honey

Blend with ice and pour.
Garnish with a sprinkle of almond flakes and nutmeg over top.
To create a special effect, drag a strand of cotton over completed cocktail.

Tequila Sunrise

Glass: 9 oz (265mL) highball glass

1 oz (30mL) tequila
1/6 oz (5mL) grenadine
Orange juice to top up

Build over ice.
Garnish with an orange wheel, a red cherry. Serve with swizzle stick and straws.
To obtain the cleanest visual effect, drop grenadine down the inside of the glass after topping up with orange juice.
Dropping grenadine in the middle creates a fallout effect, detracting from the presentation of the cocktail.
Best served with chilled, freshly squeezed oranges.

Harvey Wallbanger

Glass: 9 oz (265mL) highball glass

1 ⅓ oz (40mL) vodka
4 oz (125mL) orange juice
½ oz (15mL) Galliano, floated

Build over ice.
Garnish with an orange slice and cherry, serve with swizzle stick and straws.

Hurricane

Glass: 7 oz/210mL Hurricane Glass

1 oz (30mL) Bacardi rum
1 oz (30mL) orange juice
½ oz (15mL) lime cordial
1½ oz (45mL) lemon juice
1½ oz (45mL) sugar syrup
½ oz (15mL) Bacardi Gold to top up

Shake with ice and pour.
Garnish with orange slice and cherry. Serve with straws.

Kamikaze

Glass: 5 oz/140mL cocktail glass

1 oz (30mL) vodka
1 oz (30mL) Cointreau
1 oz (30mL) fresh lemon juice
1 tsp lime cordial

Shake with ice and strain.
Garnish with a red cocktail onion on a toothpick in the glass.
Maintain freshness for larger volumes by adding strained egg white. Mix in a jug and keep
refrigerated. For the hyper-active, Cointreau may be replaced with Triple sec.

Mai-Tai

Glass: 9 oz (265mL) highball glass

1 oz (30mL) rum
1 oz (30mL) lemon juice
½ oz (15mL) amaretto di Saronno
1 oz (30mL) sugar syrup
½ oz (15mL) rum
½ oz (15mL) fresh lime juice
1 oz (30mL) orange curacao liqueur

Shake with ice and pour.
Garnish with a pineapple spear, mint leaves, tropical flowers if possible (e.g. Singapore Orchid),
lime shell. Serve with straws.
A well-known, rum-based tropical cocktail. Grenadine is often added to give a reddening, glowing
effect, while the rum may be floated on top when served without straws. Rum lovers drink their Mai
Tais this way. It can also be built into a tall glass and stirred with the pineapple spear.

Tom Collins

Glass: 5 oz/140mL Champagne saucer

2 oz (60mL) lemon juice
2 oz (60mL) gin
Soda water to top up

Put cracked ice, lemon juice, soda water and gin in a
glass. Fill with soda water and stir. Serve with a slice of
lemon and cherry for garnish.
Brandy, bourbon, rum or any whisky can be used instead
of gin. The name changes depending on the liquor used,
eg. Rum Collins.

Zombie

Glass: 10½ oz (300mL) fancy cocktail glass

1⅓ oz (40mL) Bacardi
1 oz (30mL) dark rum
1 oz (30mL) light rum
1 oz (30mL) pineapple juice
½ oz (15mL) lime or lemon juice
1 oz (30mL) apricot brandy
1 tsp sugar syrup

Shake with ice and pour. Garnish with a pineapple spear and leaves, cherry and mint leaves. Serve with swizzle stick and straws.

Cosmopolitan

Glass: 5 oz (145mL) cocktail glass

1½ oz (45mL) vodka
1 oz (30mL) Cointreau
1 oz (30mL) cranberry juice
½ oz (15mL) freshly squeezed lime juice
Wedge of lime

Combine liquid ingredients in a cocktail shaker with cracked ice and shake well. Pour into a chilled glass. Garnish with the lime wedge.

Irish Coffee

Glass: 8 oz (250mL) Irish Coffee glass

1 oz (30mL) Baileys Irish Cream
1 tsp brown sugar
Hot black coffee to top up
Fresh cream to float

Build, no ice.
Garnish with chocolate flake (optional).
Baileys is the most widely-drunk liqueur coffee, which verifies its approval amongst coffee lovers. Tullamore Dew and Jameson are the most popular Irish whiskies. Other liqueur coffees use different spirits, such as French (brandy), English (gin), Russian (vodka), American (bourbon), Calypso (dark rum), Jamaican (Tia Maria), Parisienne (Grand Marnier), Mexican (Kahlúa), Monks (Benedictine), Scottish (Scotch) and Canadian (Rye).

Chocolate Vice

Glass: 8 oz (250mL) Irish Coffee glass

1½ oz (45mL) dark rum
½ oz (15mL) bourbon
½ oz (15mL) dark crème de cacao
4 oz (120mL) hot chocolate
2 oz (60mL) double cream
Chocolate flakes

Pour the first four ingredients into the glass, then carefully spoon cream on top. Sprinkle with chocolate flakes.

Amaretto Tea

Glass: 8 oz (250mL) Irish Coffee glass

4 oz (120mL) hot tea
2 oz (60mL) amaretto
1 tbsp whipped cream

Pour hot tea into mug and add amaretto, do not stir. Top with whipped cream.

Calypso Coffee

Glass: 8 oz (250mL) Irish Coffee glass

Slice of orange
Sugar
1½ oz (45mL) dark rum
Hot coffee
Whipped cream

Rub rim of glass with orange, and frost with sugar. Pour rum into glass and fill to within ½ in/15mm of top with the hot coffee. Cover surface to brim with whipped cream.

Moscow Mule

Glass: 10 oz (275mL) copper Moscow mug or Collins glass.

1½ oz (45mL) vodka
1 oz (30mL) lime juice
4 oz (125mL) ginger beer
Lime wedge

Combine all liquid ingredients in a mug or glass filled with clean ice cubes and stir well. Garnish with the lime wedge.

Long Island Iced Tea

Glass: 9 oz (265mL) highball glass

1 oz (30mL) vodka
1 oz (30mL) gin
1 oz (30mL) light rum
1 oz (30mL) tequila

1 oz (30mL) lemon juice
1 tsp caster sugar
4 oz (125mL) cola
lemon slice

Combine liquid ingredients, except the cola, in a cocktail shaker with cracked ice. Shake well and strain into a highball or Collins glass almost filled with clean ice cubes. Add the cola and stir well. Garnish with a lemon slice.

Black Russian

Glass: 7 oz (210mL) Old Fashioned glass

1 oz (30mL) vodka
1 oz (30mL) kahlúa

Build over ice.

Salty Dog

Glass: 9 oz (265mL) highball glass

2 tsps salt	2 oz (60mL) vodka
Lime wedge	5 oz (140mL) grapefruit juice

Place the salt in a saucer. Rub the lime wedge around the rim of a highball, then dip the glass into the salt to coat the rim. Almost fill the glass with ice cubes and pour the vodka and grapefruit juice into the glass. Stir well.

Screwdriver

Glass: 9 oz (265mL) highball glass

1½ oz (45mL) vodka
6 oz (175mL) orange juice

Combine ingredients in a highball glass filled with clean ice cubes and stir well. A Comfortable Screw is made with 1 oz (30mL) vodka, ½ oz (15mL) Southern Comfort and topped with orange juice. A Slow Comfortable Screw has the above ingredients plus the addition of ½ oz (15mL) sloe gin. A Long Slow Comfortable Screw is a longer drink served in a Collins or highball glass. A Long Slow Comfortable Screw Up Against A Wall has all of the above plus the addition of ½ oz (15mL) Galliano.

Sex on the Beach

Glass: 9 oz (265mL) highball glass

1 oz (30mL) vodka	2 oz (60mL) cranberry juice
1 oz (30mL) peach schnapps	Orange slice
2 oz (60mL) orange juice	

Combine all liquid ingredients in a glass filled with clean ice cubes and stir well. Garnish with the orange slice.

Cointreau Caipirinha

Glass: 6 oz (175mL) Prism Rocks glass

1 oz (30mL) Cointreau
¼ fresh lime or lemon cut into pieces
Crushed ice

Place lime in glass, extract juice using a muddling stick. Fill with crushed ice and add Cointreau. Stir.

Limoncello

Glass: Vodka or shot glass

10 lemons
24 oz (750mL) bottle of vodka
3 cups white sugar
4 cups water

Zest lemons and put zest into large jar. Pour vodka over zest. Cover loosely. Allow to infuse for 1 week at room temperature. After 1 week, combine sugar and water in a saucepan. Bring to a boil and boil for 15 minutes. Do not stir. Allow syrup to cool to room temperature, then stir in vodka mixture. Strain into glass bottles and seal each bottle with a cork. Age for 2 weeks at room temperature, then put bottles in the freezer. Serve icy cold in chilled vodka or shot glasses.

Pimm's No. 1 Cup

Glass: 9½ oz (285mL) highball glass

1–1½ oz (30–45mL) Pimm's No. 1 Cup
Top up with lemondade (7-up) or dry (ginger ale), or equal parts of both

Build over ice. Garnish with orange and lemon slice, cherries and cucumber skin, serve with swizzle stick and straws. A slice of orange can detract from the sweet aftertaste. Slicing the inside of the cucumber skin allows the small drops to keep the drink chilled.

Raffles Singapore Sling

Glass: 9½ oz (285mL) highball glass

1 oz (30mL) gin
1 oz (30mL) orange juice
1 oz (30mL) cherry brandy liqueur
1 oz (30mL) lime juice
½ oz (15mL) Triple sec liqueur
1 oz (30mL) pineapple juice
Dash of Angostura bitters
½ oz (15mL) Benedictine

Shake with ice and pour.
Garnish with orange slice, mint and a cherry. Serve with swizzle stick and straws.

Sangria

Glass: 6 oz (170mL) wine glass

2/3 oz (20mL) Cointreau
2/3 oz (20mL) brandy
2/3 oz (20mL) Bacardi rum
Orange, lime, lemon and strawberry pieces
Sugar syrup to taste
Spanish red wine (depending on your mixing jug or bowl - I recommend half a bottle)

Pour in order.
Thinly slice fruit and place in bowl. Pour in sugar syrup and allow to stand for several hours. Add red wine.

Rasberry Lime Punch

Serving bowl: 1 large punch bowl

16 oz (450g) raspberries
1 lime, sliced
2 tbsps sugar
2 bottles rosé wine
3 bottles Champagne

Place raspberries and lime slices into punch bowl. Sprinkle sugar over the fruit, cover and refrigerate for about half an hour. Add rosé and stir well. Add 4 cups ice cubes, then top up with the Champagne. Serve in cocktail glasses.

Old English Punch

Serving bowl: 1 large punch bowl

2 bunches mint leaves
8 oz (250mL) whiskey
2 bottles white wine
2 bottles Champagne
Selection of chopped fruit

Crumble mint leaves and place them in the bowl with 4 cups ice cubes, pour the whiskey over and let stand for about 15 minutes. Pour all other ingredients into the punch bowl and stir well. Serve in cocktail glasses.

Apple Punch

Serving Bowl: 1 large punch bowl

8 apples, cored and sliced
Juice of 1 lemon
2 tbsps sugar
4 oz (120mL) Calvados
2 bottles white wine
1 bottle soda water
1 bottle Champagne

Place apples in punch bowl, drizzle lemon juice over them and sprinkle with sugar. Refrigerate for 3–4 hours. Add Calvados and white wine and stir well. Add the soda water, Champagne and 4 cups ice cubes. Serve in cocktail glasses or Champagne flutes. Garnish with apple slices.

Gin Punch

Serving bowl: 1 large punch bowl

1 bottle gin
5 cups pineapple juice
5 cups lemonade
2 oz (60mL) lemon juice
4 cups orange juice
Selection of chopped fruit

Put all ingredients into punch bowl with 4 cups ice cubes and stir well.
Serve in punch cups.

PREPARING YOUR SHOTS

DOWN THE HATCH

Just like cocktails, constructing a shot can involve a number of different methods.

SHAKE

Half-fill a cocktail shaker with ice, then pour the ingredients in over the ice. This will chill them more quickly than pouring them in before ice. Avoid over-filling your shaker. Stand still and shake vigorously for about 10 seconds, then strain into chosen glass and serve. The majority of cocktail shakers have a strainer; if yours doesn't, buy a Hawthorn strainer. Fizzy drinks should never be shaken in a cocktail shaker. After each use, rinse the shaker out thoroughly and dry with a clean lint-free cloth. This will ensure your drinks won't have any unwanted bits in them that could distort the taste.

STIR

Half-fill a glass with ice and pour the ingredients over. Stir and strain into a serving glass. Ingredients that mix together well are prepared like this. Some shooters need ingredients to be poured directly into the glass before stirring and serving.

BUILD

Pour ingredients, in the order given in the recipe, into a chosen glass over ice and serve with a swizzle stick or straw, so the recipient may stir and admire.

LAYER

Pour ingredients in the order given in the recipe by pouring over the back of a spoon into a chosen glass. This will allow the liquid to flow down the inside rim of the glass, creating a layered effect. Heavier ingredients are usually poured first.

Lip Sip Suck

1 oz (30mL) tequila
Lemon in quarters or slices
Salt

Pour tequila into glass. Put a pinch of salt on the flat piece of skin between the base of your thumb and index finger. Place a quarter of lemon by you on the bar. Lick the salt off your hand, shoot the tequila and then suck the lemon, all in quick succession.

Chilli Shot

1½ oz (45mL) vodka
Slice of red chilli pepper

Place slice of chilli in glass, pour and shoot.
Feeling mischievous? Refrigerate the vodka with one red chilli pepper (or 3 to 5 drops of Tabasco Sauce) for 24 hours. Remove the chilli before serving with an innocent expression.

Bloody Mary Oyster Shots

12 oz (350mL) tomato juice
3¼ oz (100mL) vodka
2 tbsps lemon juice
1 tsp Worcestershire sauce
5–6 drops Tabasco
24 fresh oysters
1 Lebanese cucumber, cut into thin sticks
Salt and freshly ground black pepper

Combine tomato juice, vodka, lemon juice, Worcestershire sauce and Tabasco in a large jug. Pour mixture evenly between shot glasses. Place an oyster and a piece of cucumber in each glass and season with salt and pepper. Makes 24.

B-52

¹⁄₃ oz (10mL) Kahlúa
¹⁄₃ oz (10mL) Baileys Irish Cream
¹⁄₃ oz (10mL) Amaretto

Layer ingredients in order into a test tube and serve.

Vanilla Kiss

½ oz (15mL) vanilla schnapps
½ oz (15mL) hot cocoa
½ oz (15mL) fresh cream, chilled

Layer ingredients in order into a tall Dutch cordial glass and serve.

Lava Lamp

¼ oz (8mL) Kahlúa
¼ oz (8mL) strawberry liqueur
¼ oz (8mL) Frangelico
¼ oz (8mL) Baileys Irish Cream
3 drops advocaat liqueur

Pour Kahlúa, strawberry liqueur and Frangelico into a shot glass – do not stir. Layer Baileys on top and add advocaat by drops. Serve.

Mud Slide

½ oz (15mL) amaretto
½ oz (15mL) peppermint schnapps
½ oz (15mL) Tia Maria

Pour ingredients into a cocktail shaker over ice and shake. Strain into a chilled shot glass and serve.

Slippery Nipple

²/₃ oz (20mL) sambuca
¹/₃ oz (10mL) Baileys Irish Cream

Layer ingredients in order into a Cordial Embassy glass and serve.

Flaming Bob Marley

½ oz (15mL) 151-proof Bacardi rum
¼ oz (8mL) white crème de menthe
¼ oz (8mL) grenadine

Pour grenadine and crème de menthe into a shot glass – do not stir. Layer Bacardi on top and carefully ignite the rum by passing a lighter over it. Quickly put the straw in, plunging it to the bottom of the glass, into the grenadine syrup. The straw won't melt if it's done right.

Q.F.

$2/5$ oz (12mL) Kahlúa
$2/5$ oz (12mL) Midori
¼ oz (8 mL) Baileys Irish Cream

Layer ingredients in the order given into a Cordial Embassy glass and serve.

Apple Pie

1 oz (30mL) vodka
$1/6$ oz (5mL) cinnamon schnapps
¼ oz (8 mL) apple juice

Pour ingredients into a mixing glass over ice and stir. Strain into a chilled shot glass and serve.

Damn Good!

½ oz (15mL) butterscotch schnapps
¼ oz (8mL) green crème de menthe
¼ oz (8mL) Baileys Irish Cream
¼ oz (8mL) grenadine

Pour schnapps into a Lexington glass and layer crème de menthe on top. Layer Baileys on top and slowly add grenadine by pouring down inside rim of glass. Allow to settle on bottom of drink, then serve.

Jam Doughnut

⅔ oz (20mL) butterscotch schnapps
⅓ oz (10mL) Baileys Irish Cream
Dash of grenadine

Layer ingredients in the order given into a Cordial Embassy glass and serve.

Cock-Sucking Cowboy

1 oz (30mL) butterscotch schnapps
5mL (1/6fl oz) Baileys Irish Cream

Layer ingredients in the order given into a shot glass and serve.

PREPARING YOUR FRIENDS' ALCOHOL INTAKE

EASY DOES IT

At any party or event where alcohol is served, it's possible someone will end up a bit worse for wear. But as the host, you can do plenty to help your guests avoid nasty sore heads in the morning.

The best motto is be prepared. Fatty foods soak up alcohol and fill the stomach. Anything rich in carbohydrates and protein is perfect. Encourage everyone at your party not to drink on an empty stomach. But by the same token, don't encourage people to overeat.

Having plenty of water on hand is a must. Don't give people soft drink or juices if they are feeling too tipsy – these will keep the alcohol in your guest's system longer. Water is the best thing to give someone if they have had too much to drink.

Ask the person to stand, not sit, and encourage them to be active, such as by taking short walks. If your friend is really under the weather, a cold shower might help to sober them up.

If all else fails, send your friend to the powder room and be on standby. Sometimes it's better to get it up and out. A fresh face towel dipped in cold water is a blessing at a time like this, as is a helping hand to keep hair out of the way.

PREPARING YOUR MENU FOOD

FINGER FOOD

CRISPY STUFFED MUSHROOMS, JAPANESE PORK GYOZAS, SMOKED SALMON ROLL, CRAB RICE PAPER ROLLS, ROAST BEEF WITH CARAMELISED ONIONS, CRISPY STUFFED MUSHROOMS, JAPANESE PORK GYOZAS, SMOKED SALMON ROLL, CRAB RICE PAPER ROLLS, ROAST BEEF WITH CARAMELISED ONIONS, CRISPY STUFFED MUSHROOMS, JAPANESE PORK GYOZAS, SMOKED SALMON ROLL, CRAB RICE PAPER ROLLS, ROAST BEEF WITH CARAMELISED ONIONS, CRISPY STUFFED MUSHROOMS, JAPANESE PORK GYOZAS, SMOKED SALMON ROLL, CRAB RICE PAPER ROLLS, ROAST BEEF WITH CARAMELISED ONIONS, CRISPY STUFFED MUSHROOMS, JAPANESE PORK GYOZAS, SMOKED

61

PREPARING YOUR FOOD

It's always best to sit down and write up a menu for your event. You need to account for who is attending (including any dietary restrictions), what style of event you're having and whether you need food to match the party's theme. If there will be a lot of drinking, you should supply plenty of nibbles throughout the night.

Once you have decided whether you're having a sit-down meal, finger food, or tapas served with plates and cutlery, you need to sort out your serving dishes and platters, as well as any cutlery or tableware for the guests. These should fit in with the theme too, if you have one. I find white platters easiest to present. You can wash them up quickly and reuse them on the night if you need to. Try to work out how many serving trays you have and what food they can be used for, and count your crockery ahead of time.

Once the menu has been decided, it's a good idea to work out your timings for food preparation. You need to establish when and how long to spend preparing food the day before the event, as well as on the day, and what has to be done just before your guests arrive.

Make sure you set yourself a budget, too. It's very easy to overspend on food that you might not use. If you have a set menu, then you will know what ingredients and food to buy. These are all simple things that will help you plan a stellar menu.

If you are doing finger food, be sure to spread the food out through the night. If you think people are drinking too much then it's vital to get more food out to your guests. I have a friend who has her talented husband prepare the food in advance, and leave her very simple instructions for reheating and serving. As my friend Ollie can't boil an egg, she is a lucky girl to have a foodie for a husband. But she also knows how to dial for pizza in case her guests need more food later in the night.

If you're lucky enough to have a friend, partner or family member who will prepare the food a few hours beforehand, be sure to read their instructions carefully. You don't want to be calling your mother or your boyfriend in the middle of your girls' night to confirm how long to put the garlic bread in the oven for, or to check if that beautiful soup will need heating up.

In this chapter, you'll find lots of ideas for tapas, finger food and dips. These gorgeous recipes look and taste great, but can all be prepared with a minimum of fuss, ensuring you're able to enjoy yourself on the day or night – as well as earning major kudos for the delicious food you've supplied!

Salmon Spread

Serves 4

5 slices smoked salmon
2–3 tbsps salmon sauce
1 tbsp dill, freshly chopped
Freshly ground black pepper

FOR THE SALMON SAUCE:
3 tbsps sweet mustard
1 tbsp French mustard
1 egg yolk
2 tbsps sugar
2 tbsps white wine vinegar
7 oz (200mL) olive oil

To make the sauce, mix all sauce ingredients thoroughly. Cut the salmon into thin shreds and bind it with the sauce. Season with freshly ground pepper. Serve with crackers or chunky slices of bread and garnish with flat-leaf parsley, chopped chives or fresh dill.

Guacamole

Makes approx. 2 cups

2 tbsps onion, diced
¼ hot fresh green Serrano chillies
1 tbsp fresh coriander (cilantro)
½ tsp salt
½ tbsp lemon juice
4 avocados, peeled, seeded and mashed
2 medium-sized roma tomatoes, diced

In a food processor, blend the onion, chilli, coriander/cilantro, salt and lemon juice until smooth. Add the avocado and tomato to the blended ingredients and mix thoroughly.

Place in a serving bowl and serve with warm corn chips.

Layered Dip

Serves 8

400g (13 oz) can red kidney beans, drained and rinsed
Pepper to taste
2 small tomatoes, chopped
2 spring onions (scallions), chopped
2 small avocados, chopped
¼ cup fresh coriander (cilantro) leaves, chopped
1 small red chilli, deseeded, finely chopped
1 tbsp lime juice
½ cup grated cheese
½ cup extra light sour cream
Chopped fresh coriander (cilantro) leaves to garnish

Place the beans in a bowl. Using the back of a fork, lightly mash them and season with pepper. Stir in the tomato and spring onions/scallions.

Place avocado in a bowl. Add the coriander/cilantro, chilli and lime juice. Mash until smooth.

Place the bean mixture in the base of a medium-sized glass bowl. Put a layer of avocado mixture on top. Top with the cheese and sour cream and garnish with coriander/cilantro.

Serve with warm corn chips.

NOTE: Introduced by the Spanish, the herb cilantro is the green leaves of the coriander plant. Fresh cilantro is featured in many Mexican dishes and is a must in salsas. Cooked, it loses its taste and appearance, therefore ideally it is added to dishes just before serving.

Smoked Oyster Dip

Serves 4

4 oz (125g) cream cheese
1 spring onion (scallion), cut into 1in (25mm) lengths
1 tsp lemon juice
3½ oz (100g) canned smoked oysters
Salt and freshly-ground black pepper
1 packet crackers

In a food processor, place cream cheese, spring onion and lemon juice and beat until smooth, with spring onion finely chopped.

Add smoked oysters with oil directly from the can, with salt and pepper. Pulse in 2 second bursts until oysters are roughly chopped.

Place in serving bowl, cover and refrigerate. Serve with a selection of crackers

Nachos

Serves 4 to 6

10 cups corn chips
3 cups grated cheddar cheese
2 tbsps pickled jalapeños, chopped (optional)
2 cups tomato salsa
¾ cup guacamole (see page 66)
¾ cup sour cream
½ small red sweet pepper (capsicum) finely diced, for garnish
Spring onion (scallions), sliced, for garnish

Preheat oven to 350°F (180°C).

Place the corn chips on a large plate or casserole dish or on individual plates. Layer evenly with the cheese and sprinkle with the jalapeño. Bake in the oven for 10 to 15 minutes until all the cheese has melted evenly and is just starting to turn golden.

Remove from the oven and top with the salsa, guacamole and sour cream. Garnish with capsicum/sweet pepper and spring onions/scallions and serve immediately.

Crispy Stuffed Mushrooms

Makes 24

2 cups fresh white breadcrumbs
2 tbsp finely chopped shaved ham
1 tbsp finely chopped sun-dried tomatoes
1 tbsp sliced chives
2 tbsp melted butter
Salt and freshly ground black pepper
2 eggs, lightly beaten
24 button mushrooms, stalks removed
Vegetable oil for frying

Combine a third of a cup of breadcrumbs with the ham, sun-dried tomatoes, chives, butter, salt and pepper in a bowl.

Fill mushrooms evenly with stuffing.

Place eggs and remaining breadcrumbs in two separate bowls. Dip mushrooms into the egg and then coat in breadcrumbs.

Heat enough oil in a wok. Deep-fry mushrooms in batches for 1–2 minutes or until golden and crisp. Leave to cool a little and then serve.

Japanese Pork Gyozas

Makes 22–24

7 oz (200g) pork mince
2 shallots, sliced
½ cup chopped baby bok choy leaves
2 tsp mirin
2 tsp light soy sauce
1 tsp sesame oil
22–24 gyoza wrappers (Japanese wrappers)
2–3 tbsp peanut oil

FOR THE DIPPING SAUCE:
2 tbsp light soy sauce
2 tbsp mirin
1 tsp grated ginger

Place pork mince, shallots, bok choy, mirin, soy sauce and sesame oil in a food processor. Process until mixture is combined.

Place heaped teaspoons of mixture in the centre of each wrapper. Brush the edges lightly with water and fold over. Place dumpling upright and gently pinch the edges together. Repeat with remaining mixture and gyoza wrappers.

Line a bamboo steamer with baking paper and make holes in the paper with a skewer. Place steamer over a fry pan of boiling water. Cook in batches for 6 minutes or until just cooked. Remove and set aside.

Heat 2 tablespoons of peanut oil in a fry pan over medium heat. Fry dumplings in batches for 1–2 minutes or until crisp.

To make the dipping sauce, combine light soy sauce, mirin and ginger in a small bowl. Serve dumplings with dipping sauce.

Smoked Salmon Rolls

Makes about 24

$^1/_3$ cup light cream cheese
1 tbsp finely chopped dill
1 tbsp drained and chopped capers
1 tsp finely grated lemon zest
Salt and freshly ground black pepper
4 burrito tortillas
7 oz (200g) smoked salmon
Olive oil spray

Combine cream cheese, dill, capers, lemon zest, salt and pepper in a bowl.

Place burritos on a clean surface. Spread cheese mixture evenly over burritos. Place smoked salmon evenly down the centre of the burritos.

Roll up the burritos and spray with olive oil. Heat a nonstick fry pan over high heat. Cook burritos for 1–2 minutes, turning to brown them on all sides. Leave to cool then cut into 5–6 pieces.

Arrange smoked salmon rolls on a serving plate.

Crab Rice Paper Rolls

Makes about 22

You can substitute crab meat for 2 cups of finely shredded cooked chicken.

2 oz (60g) vermicelli noodles
1 Lebanese cucumber, halved lengthwise and seeds removed
4 shallots, thinly sliced
½ cup fresh coriander (cilantro) leaves
½ cup fresh mint leaves
10½ oz (300g) fresh crab meat or 2 cups shredded chicken
¼ cup lemon juice
2 tbsp sweet-chilli sauce
22 small rice paper sheets (about 6in/6cm round)

DIPPING SAUCE:
¼ cup sweet-chilli sauce
2 tbsp rice vinegar
2 tsp fish sauce

Cook noodles in a saucepan of boiling water for 3–4 minutes or until tender. Drain and set aside.

Cut cucumber in half again lengthwise and thinly slice. Combine noodles, shallots, cucumber, coriander (cilantro), mint, crab meat, lemon juice and sweet-chilli sauce in a bowl.

Dip each rice paper sheet in a bowl of very hot water (nearly boiling) until soft. Place four at a time on a clean surface.

Place spoonfuls of mixture on the sheets, fold in the edges and roll up. Repeat with remaining mixture and sheets.

To make the dipping sauce, combine sweet-chilli sauce, rice vinegar and fish sauce in a small bowl. Serve the rolls with the dipping sauce.

Roast Beef with Caramelised Onions

Makes about 28

2 tbsp olive oil
2 medium onions, halved and thinly sliced
1½ tbsp balsamic vinegar
1 tbsp brown sugar
1½ tbsp thyme leaves
1 french bread stick or baguette, cut into ¾in (1½cm) slices
Olive oil spray
$^1/_3$ cup light cream cheese
14 large, thin slices of rare roast beef, cut in half

Preheat oven to 440°F (220°C).

Heat oil in a saucepan over low heat. Cook onion for 10 minutes, or until soft, stirring from time to time. Add balsamic vinegar and brown sugar. Cover and cook for a further 15 minutes, or until caramelised, stirring from time to time. Transfer onions to a bowl and stir in thyme leaves.

Meanwhile place bread slices on a baking tray and spray with olive oil. Place in the oven and cook for 5–6 minutes or until just golden.

Spread bread evenly with cream cheese, top with roast beef and caramelised onions.

Chicken Liver Pâté

Serves 4

1 onion, finely chopped
1 clove garlic, finely chopped
1 rasher bacon, finely chopped
4 oz (125g) butter
8 oz (250g) chicken livers, cleaned
½ tsp fresh thyme, chopped
Salt and freshly ground black pepper
¼ cup cream
1 tbsp brandy
1 packet water crackers

Melt butter in a frypan. Add the onion, garlic and bacon, and cook until tender.

Add chicken livers, thyme, salt and pepper. Cook for a further 5 minutes.

Allow to cool slightly then place in a food processor and process until smooth.

Add brandy and cream and process until well combined.

Place into a large mould and surround with crackers.

Tapenade

Serves 6–8

10½ oz (300g) black olives
3½ oz (100g) anchovies
7 oz (200g) capers
1 crushed clove of garlic
½–1 cup olive oil
1 tsp French mustard
Lemon juice
Fresh basil, finely chopped
Freshly ground black pepper
Bread for toasting

Drain olives and remove pips. Drain anchovies. Place the olives, capers, anchovies and garlic in a blender. While the blender is running, add drops of olive oil and continue until the mix is smooth. Season with mustard, lemon, basil and black pepper.

Keep refrigerated in a glass jar and let it mature for a couple of days. Serve a spoonful of the mix onto thinly sliced bread that is brushed with olive oil and garlic, and then toasted in the oven.

NOTE: In France, tapenade is called the poor man's caviar. Tapenade can also be made with green olives.

Salmon Rolls with Horseradish Cheese

Makes approx. 20–25

8 slices of smoked salmon
3½ oz (100g) soft cheese, or cream cheese
1 tbsp minced horseradish
Chives, finely chopped
Freshly ground black pepper

Combine the cream cheese and horseradish. On a sheet of plastic wrap, slightly overlap the salmon slices. Spread with the cheese and cover with a small amount of ground black pepper. Sprinkle the finely chopped chives on top. Roll up salmon tightly and enclose in the sheet of plastic wrap. Refrigerate.

This can be prepared a few days beforehand and kept in the refrigerator. Just before serving, cut into slices.

Duck Pancakes

Makes 24

1 Chinese barbecued duck
4 spring onions (scallions), cut into thin 4in (10cm) pieces long
1 Lebanese cucumber, cut into thin 4in (10cm) pieces long
24 Chinese pancakes or burrito tortillas
Hoisin sauce to serve

Remove skin and meat from duck and slice thinly. Warm pancakes or burritos according to packet directions.

Divide duck, spring onions and cucumber evenly between pancakes. Spoon over a little hoisin sauce and fold over pancakes. You may need toothpicks to hold them together for serving. Serve warm.

You can substitute Chinese pancakes for burrito tortillas and cut them into quarters.

Chinese Chicken Drumettes

Makes 24

24 small chicken wings
2 tbsps vegetable oil
3 tbsps hoisin sauce
4 tbsps light soy sauce
2 tbsps dry sherry
4 cloves garlic, crushed
1 small red chilli pepper, seeded and chopped
3 tsps peeled and grated fresh ginger
½ cup additional hoisin sauce, for dipping

Cut chicken wings in half at main joint. Discard wing tips (or save for making stock). With a sharp knife, trim meat around each cut joint, then scrape meat down the bone and push it over the bottom joint so the wing resembles a small chicken leg. Place drumettes in a shallow dish.

Combine oil, 3 tablespoons hoisin sauce, soy sauce, sherry, garlic, chili and ginger in a screw-top jar. Shake until well combined. Pour over chicken. Cover and marinate in refrigerator for 3 hours.

Preheat oven to 350°F (180°C). Remove chicken from marinade and place in a lightly greased baking dish. Bake in preheated oven until tender, 15–20 minutes.

Serve hot or cold, with hoisin sauce for dipping.

Lamb Meatballs with Tzatziki

Makes about 40

FOR THE MEATBALLS:
15 oz (450g) minced/ground lamb
1 tsp ground coriander
1 tsp ground cumin
Pinch of chilli
1 tbsp tomato paste
1 bunch cilantro (coriander), chopped
Grated zest of 1 lemon
Salt and freshly ground black pepper
Oil for frying

FOR THE TZATZIKI:
1 cucumber, deseeded
2 cups natural yoghurt
1–2 garlic cloves, crushed
1 tbsp mint, chopped
Salt and freshly ground black pepper

To make the lamb meatballs, mix all ingredients except the oil together with the mince and season to taste. Shape the mince into small meatballs. Fry in oil until they are cooked through and golden brown.

To make the tzatziki, grate cucumber coarsely, add salt and drain in a colander. Pour the yoghurt into a coffee filter and let it drain for a couple of hours. Remove from filter into a bowl, and mix yoghurt, cucumber, crushed garlic and chopped mint. Season to taste with salt and pepper. Serve in a bowl alongside the meatball with toothpicks.

Smoked Salmon Canapés

Makes 24

½ cup cream cheese
1 tbsp horseradish cream
1 tbsp chives, thinly sliced
6 slices rye bread, cut into quarters
7 oz (200g) smoked salmon, sliced
Baby capers to garnish

Combine cream cheese, horseradish cream and chives in a small bowl. Spread bread evenly with cream cheese mixture. Top with smoked salmon and garnish with capers.

Marinated Stuffed Mushrooms

Makes 24

24 button mushrooms
2 tbsps olive oil
¼ cup lemon juice
3 hardboiled eggs, mashed
2 tbsps sour cream
¼ bunch chives, sliced
Salt and freshly ground black pepper
Red or black caviar, to garnish

Brush dirt from mushrooms and remove stalks. Combine oil and lemon juice in a bowl. Add mushrooms and toss well. Leave to marinate for about 3 hours or until softened a little.

Drain mushrooms and wipe with a paper towel so the mushrooms are not slippery and greasy. Combine eggs, sour cream, chives, salt and pepper in a bowl. Fill mushroom cavities with egg mixture and top with a little caviar.

When purchasing mushrooms, make sure you choose really fresh ones that are firm and white in appearance. The older the mushroom, the more lemon juice it absorbs, which overpowers the dish.

Cherry Tomatoes with Artichokes

Makes about 60

1lb (500g) cherry tomatoes

FOR THE ARTICHOKE FILLING:
14 oz (400g) artichoke hearts
4 oz (125g) Parmesan cheese, grated
1 cup mayonnaise
¼ cup fresh parsley, chopped

Cut a slice off the bottom of each washed tomato. Carefully remove the seeds and allow the tomatoes to drain upside down on paper towels.

Drain the artichoke hearts. In a blender or food processor chop them finely. Add the cheese and mayonnaise to the artichokes and blend well.

Fill each tomato using either a pastry bag fitted with a large tip or a very small spoon. Cover the tomatoes and refrigerate.

The tomatoes may be served at room temperature, or heated for five minutes in a 200°F (100°C) preheated oven. Garnish with a sprinkle of chopped parsley.

Mini Hamburgers

Makes 12

1 egg
7 oz (200g) lean beef mince
2 oz (50g) chopped onion
1 tsp crushed garlic
Salt and freshly ground black pepper
1 tsp chutney
1 tsp tomato sauce
¼ cup flour
Vegetable oil for frying
12 mini-hamburger rolls, halved and buttered
Gherkins, lettuce, cocktail tomatoes and mustard

Mix all the ingredients up to and including tomato sauce. Shape into small patties and coat with flour.

Heat oil in a heavy-based saucepan and fry the patties. Drain on kitchen paper. Place a patty on the bottom half of each roll.

Top with sliced gherkin, shredded lettuce, tomato halves and a dollop of mustard. Carefully replace the top half of each roll.

Salt-and-Spice Almonds

Serves 3–4

6 tbsps vegetable oil
14 oz (440 g) whole blanched almonds
2 tbsps sea salt
½ tsp ground cayenne pepper, or to taste

In a medium frying pan over medium heat, warm oil. Add almonds and cook, tossing or stirring constantly, until they just become golden, around 1–2 minutes. Be careful; almonds can burn easily at the last minute.

Combine sea salt and cayenne pepper in a bowl. Add hot almonds and toss until well coated. Place almonds on a parchment-lined (baking paper–lined) baking sheet and allow to cool. Serve with drinks.

The almonds can be made 3–4 days ahead of time. Once they have completely cooled, store in an airtight container.

Crisp Vegetable Chips

Serves 6–8

6 cups vegetable oil
3 sweet potatoes (kumaras), peeled
4 potatoes, peeled
4 parsnips, peeled
3 beets (beetroots), peeled
5 tsps sea salt, or to taste

Heat oil in a large, deep, heavy-bottomed saucepan or deep-fat fryer until it reaches 375°F (190°C) on a deep-frying thermometer, or until a small cube of bread dropped into the oil sizzles and turns golden. Working with one vegetable at a time (reserve beets until last as they make the oil red), thinly slice each vegetable using a vegetable peeler or mandoline.

Working with handful-sized batches, add vegetable slices to hot oil and deep-fry until golden, about 1 minute. Using a slotted spoon, remove from oil and drain on paper towels.

Sprinkle the chips liberally with sea salt and serve immediately.

Parmesan Wafers

Makes about 20

10½ oz (300g) freshly grated parmesan cheese

Preheat oven to 350°F (180°C). Working in batches, place tablespoonfuls of cheese onto parchment-lined (baking paper–lined) baking sheets, allowing space for spreading. Flatten each mound into a 2-inch (5-cm) round, or until it is almost paper thin. Bake until golden, 8–10 minutes.

Remove baking sheets from oven. Using a metal spatula, remove wafers from sheets and place on a parchment-lined (baking paper–lined) rolling pin or similar curved shape. Allow to cool. Serve warm or at room temperature.

Blini Bites with Salmon Roe

Makes about 24

1¼ cups self-rising flour
Pinch of baking soda (bicarbonate of soda)
1 egg, beaten
¾ cup milk
1 tbsp grated white onion
Sea salt and freshly ground black pepper to taste
2 tbsps butter, melted
½ cup crème fraîche or sour cream
4 oz (125g) salmon roe

Place flour and baking soda in a food processor. Add egg and milk. Process until smooth. Transfer batter to a bowl. Add grated onion, salt and pepper. Mix well. Cover and let stand for 10 minutes.

Heat a frying pan over medium heat, and brush with melted butter. Drop batter by the tablespoonful into hot pan. Cook until golden, about 1 minute per side. Remove from pan and allow to cool to room temperature.

Just before serving, top each blini with crème fraîche and a small amount of salmon roe.

Sun-Dried Tomato–Filled Toast Cups

Makes 30

15 large slices white sandwich bread
Olive oil, for brushing
4 oz (125g) sun-dried tomatoes in oil, drained and chopped
4 oz (125g) freshly grated parmesan cheese
10½ oz (300g) ricotta cheese
2 tbsps chopped fresh parsley
Sea salt and freshly ground black pepper to taste
Small herb leaves such as basil, parsley or thyme, for garnish

Preheat oven to 375°F (190°C). Remove crusts from bread with a serrated bread knife. Roll bread flat using a rolling pin. Cut rounds from bread using a 2-inch (5-cm) cookie (pastry) cutter. Brush one side of bread rounds with oil. Press bread rounds, oiled side up, into greased mini muffin pans. Bake in preheated oven until golden and crisp, 5–7 minutes.

Meanwhile, prepare the filling. In a bowl, combine sun-dried tomatoes, parmesan, ricotta, parsley, salt and pepper. Mix until well combined.

Remove pans from oven when ready, then remove toast cups from pans and allow to cool. Spoon cheese mixture into toast cups, and garnish with herb leaves.

Endive Leaves with Herbed Cheese and Walnuts

Serves 8–10

4 heads Belgian endive (chicory/witloof)
8 oz (250g) ricotta cheese
¼ cup chopped fresh parsley
¼ cup chopped fresh dill
1 garlic clove, crushed
Freshly ground black pepper to taste
Walnut pieces, for garnish

Separate Belgian endive leaves, then wash and pat dry with paper towels. Trim bottom of each leaf. Using a wooden spoon or fork, blend ricotta, parsley, dill, garlic and pepper in a small bowl. Spoon a small amount on each leaf – not too much to make it difficult for the leaf to hold the filling. Garnish with walnut pieces and serve.

Chilled Gazpacho Sips

Makes 16 servings, about 1½ oz (45mL) each.

1 hothouse (English) cucumber
½ Spanish (red) onion, chopped
1 ripe tomato, finely chopped
½ green capsicum (bell pepper), seeded and chopped
½ red capsicum (bell pepper), seeded and chopped
3½ cups canned tomato juice
1 tsp superfine sugar (caster sugar)
3 tbsps dry white wine
3 cloves garlic, crushed

Cut cucumber in half lengthwise. Scoop out seeds, using a teaspoon. Finely chop one half of cucumber. Cut remaining half into thin slivers for garnish, cover and set aside.

Combine chopped cucumber, onion, tomato and bell peppers in a bowl and set aside. Combine tomato juice, sugar, white wine and garlic in a pitcher. Chill for at least 2 hours, or until ready to serve.

To serve, pour juice mixture into 16 shot glasses, then spoon in vegetable mixture. Garnish each glass with a thin sliver of cucumber.

PREPARING YOUR PIZZA NIGHT

MAMMA MIA!

Who doesn't love pizza? With its endless options for toppings, it can be tailored to anyone's taste or dietary preferences and is also fun to make.

Making your own dough might seem like a challenge you don't want to take up, but it's a much easier process than people think. It can, however, take some time. Make the dough that day, before the event, or a few days earlier and freeze it. Then when you're ready to use it you only have to roll it out, pop your desired ingredients on top and bake. You could even make pizza preparations a party activity for the group to do together.

Have a go at making your own dough (page 120). Remember to give your yeast time to absorb in the water, and your dough plenty of time to raise and double in size in a warm area of your kitchen.

Alternatively you can buy pizza bases and add your preferred sauces and toppings as you please. In this chapter, we have included a classic base sauce (page 123), but you can buy these easily at any food store. Toppings, meanwhile, can be whatever you feel like, in any combination of meat, seafood, vegetables and cheeses.

My husband loves a huge amount of toppings on his pizza but I prefer a small amount, so when I make pizza at home I use less cheese and toppings on one side, and more on the other side for my husband. Pizza is so easy to adapt to your taste.

Whatever method you choose, it will be a crowd-pleasing menu option for your night with the girls.

Basic Pizza Dough

Makes 1 pizza crust • Preparation 1 hour

1½ tsps dry yeast
Pinch of sugar
1⅓ cups warm water (about 105°F/41°C)
½ cup olive oil
4 cups plain flour, sifted
1¼ tsps salt
Olive oil for bowl, as needed

In a small bowl dissolve yeast and sugar in the warm water and let stand 5 minutes. Stir in olive oil. In a large bowl combine flour and salt. Add yeast mixture and stir until dough just barely holds together.

Turn dough out onto a lightly floured surface and knead until smooth and silky, adding a little more flour if dough seems sticky. Put dough in an oiled bowl and turn to coat surface with oil. Cover bowl with cling wrap and let rise in a warm place until it has doubled in bulk (about 1 hour).

Once dough has doubled, punch it down, using your fist in a straight-down motion.

To shape into pizza crust, on a lightly floured surface roll dough out to desired size. Place the dough on a baker's peel or oiled pizza pan dusted with cornmeal. Any excess dough can be wrapped in plastic kitchen wrap and kept in the refrigerator.

A simple, straightforward dough enriched with oil, this is ready to use in a little more than an hour. For a firm, elastic dough that yields a crisp, finely textured crust, replace up to half the flour with semolina, a high-protein flour ground from hard durum wheat.

Basic Tomato Sauce

Makes about 1½ cups • Preparation 30 minutes • Cooking 20 minutes

¼ cup fresh basil, chopped
½ tsp dried oregano
1½ tbsps white wine
¼ medium onion, grated
1 clove garlic, chopped
1 tsp olive oil
2 tomatoes peeled, deseeded and chopped
1½ tsps tomato paste

In a small bowl, steep basil and oregano in white wine for 10 minutes.

In a frying pan over medium-high heat, sauté onion and garlic in olive oil for 5 minutes, stirring frequently. Add tomatoes and tomato paste, then steeped herbs and wine. Cover, reduce heat and simmer 15 minutes.

Remove sauce from heat and purée in a blender or food processor.

The secret to the taste of this quick, low-fat sauce, which uses very little oil, is steeping the basil and oregano in wine before cooking. This simple step draws out the taste of the herbs, creating a sauce that tastes as if it had been cooking for hours. This recipe calls for fresh tomatoes, but you may also use canned tomatoes.

Spicy Pizza Sauce

Makes about 2 cups • Preparation 15 minutes • Cooking 25 minutes

1 tbsp olive oil
½ onion, finely chopped
½ red capsicum (bell pepper), chopped
1 clove garlic, chopped
1 tsp chilli flakes
1 small red chilli, chopped
14 oz (400g) canned chopped tomatoes
2 tbsps tomato paste
1 tsp dried oregano

In a saucepan, heat oil over medium heat, add onion, capsicum (bell pepper) and garlic. Cook, stirring often until the ingredients are soft.

Mix in chilli flakes, chilli, tomatoes, tomato paste and oregano. Bring to the boil and cover for about 15 minutes.

Uncover, increase the heat and stir for 10 minutes or so, or until the sauce thickens and reduces to about 2 cups,

Garlic-Oregano Pizza

Makes about 1 cup • Preparation 10 minutes • Cooking 30 minutes

6 cloves young garlic, finely chopped
1/4 cup fresh oregano, chopped
1/2 cup dry white wine
1/2 cup olive oil
Salt and freshly ground black pepper
Freshly grated Parmesan cheese

In a small saucepan over low heat, cook garlic, wine and half the olive oil until garlic is very soft (about 30 minutes). The mixture will have the consistency of a rough paste.

Spread the paste on the pizza dough. Drizzle with remaining olive oil and sprinkle with oregano. Season with salt, pepper and Parmesan cheese.

Sausage Pizza

Makes 1 • Preparation 15 minutes • Cooking 30 minutes

12 oz (340g) Italian sausage meat
Olive oil
1 quantity deep-dish pizza dough (see page 120)
5 oz (150g) mozzarella cheese, grated
8 oz (250g) mushrooms, thinly sliced
1 quantity spicy pizza sauce (see page 124)
1 oz (30g) Parmesan cheese, grated

Preheat oven to 450°F (230°C).

Crumble sausage meat into a large frying pan over medium-high heat. Cook, stirring often, until lightly browned. Pour off drippings and discard. Set sausage aside.

Oil a 15in (37cm) deep-dish pizza pan and line with dough. Sprinkle half of the mozzarella over the dough. Cover with an even layer of mushrooms, then with cooked sausage. Spread the sauce over sausage. Cover with remaining mozzarella and top with Parmesan cheese.

Bake on lowest rack of oven until crust browns well (20–25 minutes). Serve at once.

Vegetable Pizza

Makes 2 • Preparation 2 hours • Cooking 20 minutes

½ butternut pumpkin, peeled, cut into ½in (12mm) cubes
1 red capsicum (bell pepper), cut into ½in (12mm) pieces
1 yellow capsicum (bell pepper), cut into ½in (12mm) pieces
1 red (Spanish) onion, sliced
3 small zucchini (courgettes), sliced
2 tbsps olive oil
2 tsps balsamic vinegar
Salt and freshly ground black pepper
1 quantity basic pizza dough (see page 120)
½ cup tomato passata
4 oz (125g) feta, crumbled
1/3 cup basil leaves

Preheat oven to 400°F (200°C).

In a large bowl, toss pumpkin, capsicums (peppers), onion and zucchini (courgettes) with oil, then season.

In a large baking tray, fit vegetables in a single layer. Roast for 10 minutes, then place zucchini in the oven with the other vegetables for 10 minutes or until pumpkin is tender and capsicums are a little charred at the edges. Place all vegetables in a large bowl and toss with balsamic, then set aside.

Divide dough in half and roll each half out to make two 8in (20cm) circles. Wipe baking tray clean and place bases on tray. Spread passata on bases and top with vegetables, reserving any balsamic.

Top with feta and bake for 15–20 minutes until feta is golden. Toss basil in reserved balsamic and scatter over pizzas to serve.

Gorgonzola and Prosciutto Pizza

Makes 1 • Preparation 15 minutes • Cooking 20 minutes

3 cloves garlic, unpeeled
1 quantity pizza dough (see page 120)
1 quantity basic tomato sauce (see page 123)
7 oz (200g) mozzarella cheese, grated
1½ oz (45g) crumbled Gorgonzola cheese, crumbled
4 oz (125g) sliced prosciutto, cut into strips

Preheat oven to 450°F (230°C).

Add garlic to 2 cups boiling water in a small saucepan and boil for 1 minute. Drain, peel, then slice garlic thinly.

Shape pizza dough and spread sauce over the dough. Sprinkle with garlic, then with mozzarella and Gorgonzola cheeses. Arrange prosciutto strips over cheeses.

Bake on lowest rack of oven until crust is well-browned (15–20 minutes). Serve hot.

Chicken Satay Pizza

Makes 1 • Preparation 10 minutes • Cooking 22 minutes

14 oz (400g) chicken thigh fillets, diced
¾ cup satay marinade
1 tbsp peanut oil
4 spring onions (scallions), sliced
1 carrot, grated
3 oz (90g) snow peas, trimmed and sliced
1 large pizza base
2 tsps sesame seeds
¼ cup fresh coriander leaves, chopped

Preheat the oven to 430°F (220°C).

Combine the chicken with half a cup of marinade in a bowl (leaving one-quarter cup aside).

Heat the oil in a large frying pan over medium to high heat. Cook the chicken for 5 minutes. Stir in the spring onions, carrot and snow peas and cook for 1–2 minutes or until the snow peas turn bright green.

Spread the remaining marinade over the pizza base and spoon the chicken over. Sprinkle with sesame seeds. Place on a baking tray and bake for 12–15 minutes. Top with the coriander leaves and cut into wedges.

If you prefer to make your own satay marinade, heat all of the following ingredients in a pan, stir to combine, then allow to cool: ½ cup peanut butter, ½ teaspoon chilli powder, 2 tablespoons lemon juice, 1 tablespoon brown sugar, ½ teaspoon ground ginger, ½ cup coconut milk.

Ham and Mozzarella Pizza

Makes 1 • Preparation 40 minutes • Cooking 15 minutes

1 quantity basic pizza dough (see page 120)
2 tbsps olive oil
1 onion, finely chopped
4 large tomatoes, skinned and finely chopped
1 bay leaf
1 small sprig thyme
A few drops of Tabasco sauce
1 clove garlic, finely chopped
Salt and freshly ground black pepper

FOR TOPPING:
2 tomatoes, sliced
½ onion, thinly sliced
2 slices lean cooked ham, cut into small pieces
7 oz (200g) mozzarella cheese
Salt and freshly ground black pepper
1 tsp dried oregano
Fresh oregano, chopped

Preheat oven to 430°F (220°C). To make the tomato sauce, heat the oil in a frying pan and fry the onion until softened. Add the tomatoes, bay leaf, thyme, Tabasco and garlic. Season with salt and pepper and cook for about 30 minutes, stirring frequently.

When the liquid from the tomatoes has almost evaporated, remove and discard the bay leaf and the sprig of thyme. Allow the sauce to cool a little, then blend in a food processor until smooth. Roll out the dough into a round, place on a baking tray and spread with the tomato sauce.

Lay the sliced tomatoes over the tomato sauce, then top with the onion and ham. Cut the cheese into thin slices and lay the slices over the pizza. Season with salt and pepper and sprinkle over the oregano.

Bake for about 15 minutes. Serve immediately, garnished with fresh oregano.

Bacon and Goat Cheese Pizza

Makes 1 • Preparation 20 minutes • Cooking 15 minutes

1 quantity basic pizza dough (see page 120)
1 quantity basic tomato sauce (page 123)
1 onion, thinly sliced
4 rashers bacon
Salt and freshly ground black pepper
6 sprigs fresh marjoram, leaves removed and stalks discarded
Black olives
Goat cheese to taste

Preheat oven to 430°F (220°C). Roll out the dough thinly on a lightly floured work surface. Place on a buttered baking tray.

Spread the tomato sauce over the dough, then sprinkle over the onion. Cut the bacon into small pieces and scatter over the pizza. Thinly slice the goat cheese and place the slices over the bacon.

Season with salt and pepper, sprinkle over the marjoram and bake for about 15 minutes. Serve hot, garnished with olives.

PREPARING YOUR NIGHT'S PLAYLIST

FINE-TUNING

With your menu and drinks sorted, you now need music to set the scene!

It's important to plan what kind of music will suit your event. If it's a night when everyone wants to talk – and what woman doesn't love to do that? – then pick songs that won't drown out the conversation. If you want everyone up and dancing, you'll need energetic party anthems.

Also consider your theme. If you're having a pamper session, you are likely to want soft, soothing music that flows smoothly from one track to the next. For a sexy hen's night, raunchy dance songs will be better suited to the atmosphere, while a retro tea party will go perfectly with classic soul and blues. It's a good idea to divide your music up into more low-key tunes while everyone is arriving and being introduced, before pumping up the volume for dancing, then softening the mood again if you are going to be opening gifts or having speeches.

iPods and MP3 players, and streaming services like Spotify, make putting together a playlist really easy – just search for the tunes you love and you're set to download or play them, and arrange them in the order that suits you. Make a list of songs on your phone or online, and ask others for suggestions, especially if you are hosting for a friend.

Put one person in charge of the music to avoid too many guests trying to play DJ and jumping from song to song. You might enlist the talents of a professional, or you could hire a jukebox with a selection of songs – that way everyone can have a turn selecting songs.

PREPARING YOUR NIGHT'S GAMES

PLAY ALONG

There's nothing like a few games to break the ice and get people in the party mood. Add some alcohol and before you know it the festivities are in full swing. Here are some ideas for games that will suit all different kinds of events.

GUESSING GAMES

These are easy to plan and don't require more equipment than a pen and paper. For 'Who Am I?', simply write the names of famous people on slips of paper, place them in a hat, then have guests select a name, but not look at it. Divide group into pairs, swap names, and set a time limit for each person to guess their celebrity by asking their partner questions. Variations on this game include putting a nametag on each person's back, which others can see but they can't, or on a hat or headband. Guests need to solve their identity before the end of the party.

REVERSE STRIP POKER

Ask guests to bring quirky items of clothing, such as wigs, funny glasses and hats. Whenever they lose a hand at poker (or any other game you choose), they have to put an item of clothing on. The loser is the person wearing so many articles of clothing they can't fit anything else.

TEXT AND GO SEEK

One guest has to hide, then texts the seekers a picture that gives a clue as to their whereabouts, for example a picture of a shoe if they are in a wardrobe, or a clothes hamper if they are in a laundry.

TWO TRUTHS AND A LIE

Each person gives three statements about themselves, two of them true and one a lie. Everyone has to guess which is the lie.

THE SELF-PORTRAIT GAME

Each player gets an unlined piece of paper and a pencil. Turn off the lights and give everyone a minute or two to draw a self-portrait in the darkness. When the time is up, turn the lights back on and collect the drawings. Hold each portrait up and let everyone guess who the artist is. The winner is the person who correctly matches the most portraits to artists.

SCAVENGER HUNT

Divide the guests into two teams. Give each team a list of common household and personal items they need to find, such as sunglasses, clothes pegs, a pair of gloves, a baby photo, a bra, etc. The first team to assemble everything on the list wins. This game can also be played if you are out on the town, in which case items could include a photo taken with a fireman or policeman, a business card from a sexy stranger, a tie, a lemon, or a fake tattoo.

THE PEG GAME

Every guest has to wear a pre-agreed number of pegs, between five and 10, on their clothes. Come up with five words that are not allowed to be said throughout the night, for example your name, 'party', 'phone', 'shoes' and 'drink'. For more complicated fun, words can be tailored to individual guests. Anyone who overhears a banned word can remove a peg from her clothes and attach it to the rule-breaker, or vice versa. The goal can be to acquire as many pegs as possible or to get rid of your pegs. This can easily be coupled with a drinking game.

POP THE BALLOON GAME

Make a list of funny dares, enough for each person, and write them on slips of paper. Put each piece of paper in a balloon, then blow the balloons up. Each guest is given a balloon, which they will have to pop. They then have to perform the dare inside, which can be as silly or embarrassing as you like!

YES OR NO?

Form a circle with your seats. Everyone should mark their chair in some way to help remember whose is whose. Put forward a number of questions, like 'Have you ever been on TV?' or 'Have you ever met a famous person?' Each player whose answer is yes must move to the next available seat on her right. If only one player stands up, they sit back down in the same seat and don't get to move. The winner is the first person to make it back to her own seat. To make the game longer, add a few empty seats. If you have empty seats available, you may choose to allow people to move even if they are the only person to stand. The empty seats give them somewhere to move to.

BLIND TRUST MAKEOVER

In this game, one person wears a blindfold and the makeup is laid out in front of her. Another girl sits in front of the one who is blindfolded. The blindfolded player tries to put makeup on the other girl. Everyone takes a turn and admires the crazy results.

DRINKING GAMES

Drinking games are lots of fun, especially as everyone starts to get tipsier. One of the most popular drinking games is 'I never…' In this game, a person starts with a statement about something they have never done, for example, 'I have never had a one night stand.' Everyone who has done it has to drink. Depending on what you know about your friends, and what they are prepared to admit, this game can get very funny and quite revealing.

Mr (or Ms) Freeze can be played throughout the entire party. One person is designated Ms Freeze. At any point during the party, she freezes, and everyone must follow suit. The last person to catch on has to take a shot and a new Ms. Freeze is chosen.

PREPARING YOUR NIGHT'S TOPICS

THE GIRLS ONLY Q&A

Conversation cards are all the rage and it's easy to see why. If you have assembled a group of people who don't all know each other, such as a hen's party that includes family, friends and work colleagues, an easy way to break the ice is to distribute conversation cards. Go around the group with each person asking a question – or as the host, you might act as 'quiz master', drawing questions out of a hat and putting them to different guests. Combine with a drinking game for ever more entertaining answers!

SPARKLING CONVERSATION STARTERS

If you were granted three wishes, what would they be?

If you were a Disney princess, which one would it be and why?

What's the longest you've gone without food/sleep? Why?

What's the best costume you've ever worn?

If you could travel anywhere in the world, where would it be and why?

Who has been the most influential person in your life?

What was the most terrifying moment in your life?

What is the strangest thing you've ever eaten?

If you could live at any time in history, when would it be and why?

If you could have one superpower, what would it be and why?

What has been your worst hair disaster?

What's your dream job? Dream holiday?

What person would you most like to meet and why?

If it were an Olympic sport, I'd get a gold medal for …

What would you do if you won the lottery?

What would be the title of your autobiography?

If you could date anyone, who would it be?

If you could swap your life for that of someone famous, who would it be?

Do you lie about your age?

What's the most embarrassing thing you've done in public?

Have you ever stolen anything?

Have you ever Googled yourself?

Have you ever faked a sick day?

Do you have a tattoo?

Would you take revenge on a lover who cheated on you?

Would you sleep with your boss for a promotion?

Have you had an office affair?

Have you ever been fired?

If you could be invisible for half an hour, what would you do?

If you could change one thing about yourself, what would it be?

If you could go back in time, what wouldn't you have done?

Have you ever had an inappropriate crush? If so, on who?

RISKY TOPICS

Have you had sex in a public place? Where?

Have you ever cheated?

Have you faked an orgasm?

Have you faked a headache to get out of sex?

Have you had sex and thought about somebody else?

Would you ever date one of your friends exes?

Do you think size really matters?

Are you bored with your sex life?

Have you had a threesome?

Have you batted for the other team?

Do you believe in abortion?

Do you believe in God?

Have you hired a prostitute?

Have you ever been a cougar?

Are you still hung up on an ex?

What's the kinkiest thing you've done in bed?

What's the best/worst sex you've ever had?

PREPARING YOUR NIGHT'S THEMES

TIPS AND IDEAS

Whatever your celebration, choosing a theme makes it easier to plan your menu, dress code, decorating ideas, drinks and entertainment. Here are ten delightful party themes to get your girls only do off to a great start.

GODDESSES

This works really well for a hen's night, as you can celebrate your friend's impending nuptials with fortune-telling, love potions and spells for luck, happiness and prosperity. Light candles and burn incense, fill your house with flowers, and have lots of props on hand for your guests, such as wands, fairy wings and tiaras. Do tarot, palm, crystal ball and tea leaf readings. Reseach some spells for romance or prosperity, buy ingredients and create some magic. Have fortune cookies on hand or create your own.

SINGLE AND LOVING IT

Any time of year is a great time to celebrate the fabulousness of your single ladies. Dress up for a night of gourmet finger food and sophisticated cocktails. You might host a life drawing class, complete with nude model, then give prizes for the best art work. Or if you're into matchmaking, plan a dinner party where each single gal brings a single man. Celebrate the power of female friendships with a 'Sex and the City' marathon, or movies like 'Thelma & Louise' and 'Bridesmaids'.

DANCE OFF

A girls only night is the perfect opportunity to let go of any inhibitions. Book a professional dancer for some pole or striptease dance classes, or grab a pile of 'how to' DVDs. There's plenty to choose from, including burlesque, belly dancing and Bollywood. Go-go dancing is very popular, with 60s costumes and beehive hairdos. Get inspired with movies like 'Dirty Dancing' and 'Magic Mike'.

BEAUTIFY

Facials, manicures and pedicures are easy to do and relatively inexpensive. Ask guests to bring a nice fluffy towel and a luxurious bathrobe for a real day-spa effect. Create your own face masks using natural ingredients like oatmeal and avocado (there are plenty of recipes online) and ask your guests to bring one beauty item each, such as a gorgeous nail polish or mascara, so you can do makeovers on each other. Choose romantic movies like 'Jane Eyre', 'The Notebook' or 'Titanic'. Keep drinks light and fruity – Champagne or daiquiris – and provide canapés that are easy to eat with one freshly-manicured hand.

CLOTHES SWAP

Everyone has clothes they don't wear anymore (or never wore at all), but one woman's trash is another's treasure. Clothes swap parties are a great way to clean out your wardrobe and score something new. Ask friends to bring stylish clothes in good condition, then start swapping. Donate any leftovers to charity. Best movie choices: 'The Devil Wears Prada', 'Breakfast at Tiffany's', 'Marie Antoinette' and 'Sex and The City'.

GROWN-UP KIDS PARTY

The games and food you loved as a child can be a great nostalgia trip. Ask your guests to bring a picture of themselves as a child and pin them on a board for everyone to match with the grown-up version. Play pass the parcel and musical chairs, and serve mini pies and frankfurters. Blow up lots of balloons, give out party hats, and invite a magician along to do tricks. Finish the party with a big cake and give guests sweetie bags to take home with them.

RETRO

To channel serious 'Mad Men' style, embrace the dress code of a 1950s housewife, with white gloves, vintage dresses and adorable kitten heels. Bake cakes, scones and cookies and serve them on vintage crockery, cheaply available at second-hand shops along with kitsch table decorations. Mix classic cocktails like Old-Fashioneds, Sidecars and Manhattans and get a hair or makeup artist in to do some retro makeovers (or do it yourself using how-to videos online). Listen to Nat King Cole and The Beatles for a relaxed retro vibe.

SLUMBER PARTY

Remember how much fun they were? Staying up late, telling scary stories, holding séances? Get into your PJs and bring a sleeping bag. Make your own gourmet pizzas and watch scary movies. Play games like Truth and Dare, or I Never. Serve coffee, fresh juice and pastries for breakfast.

WINE TASTING

For something more sophisticated, invite the girls around for a wine and food matching party. Most wine-makers share tasting notes on their websites, so set a price and nominate a wine for each of your guests to bring, then match them with food. Have lots of bread, cheese and fruit platters, and fondue on hand, to soak up the wine.

FANCY DRESS

Costumes are a great conversation starter for people who don't know each other. Try a Bollywood theme, with Indian food and music to match, a glam high rollers party with a roulette wheel and card games, or a best of the 80s bash. Have a safari party and ask your friends to wear animal print, or to pick superheroes or historical figures. Host a diva party, with everyone coming as a popular singer, and have a contest for the best song performance in character.

HIGH TEA

Parties don't have to involve expensive food menus and masses of alcohol – why not host a high tea, and ask your guests to contribute a plate? Serve tea and coffee in pretty china tea cups and saucers, with delicate cupcakes and cucumber sandwiches. Have a garden party on the lawn or in a local park, with plenty of throw rugs, cushions and recliners. This makes for a perfect baby shower. Serve ladylike drinks such as Champagne punch or Pimms, in tall glasses with lots of ice.

PREPARING YOUR NIGHT'S MAN JOKES

LOL

Men are like horoscopes. They always tell you what to do, but are usually wrong.

How many men does it take to change a toilet roll? We don't know, it's never happened.

Men are like vacations. They never seem to be long enough.

What do men and beer have in common? They're both empty from the neck up.

Men are like laxatives. They irritate the shit out of you.

What do you give a man who has everything? A woman to show him how to work it.

How can you tell if a man is aroused? He's breathing.

Why are all dumb blonde jokes one-liners? So men can understand them.

What's the smartest thing a man can say? My wife says ...

What did God say after creating man? I can do better.

Why do men want to marry virgins? They can't stand criticism

Why do men name their penises? Because they want to be on a first-name basis with the one who makes all their decisions.

What is a man's idea of foreplay? A half-hour of begging.

Why is a man different from a PC? You only have to tell the PC once.

What's the difference between men and government bonds? Bonds mature.

PREPARING YOUR NIGHT'S SEX TALK

DIRTY MINDS

Let's talk about sex, baby! The subject of sex comes up more than you would think at a girls only event. Conversation often turns this way when girls get together, especially after a few cocktails. It's like they say – sex sells. And sex talk sells, too, as a fun way to gossip about others.

You will want to join in with your guests in these conversations, but hosting duties can be a good get-out clause if you ever want to step back. If you're talking about your sex life, you should be prepared for anything you say to be repeated. Avoid naming names, if you can, and enjoy any naughty anecdotes as light-hearted fun with the girls. Most will have some hilarious, sexy or toe-curling stories to share!

See our conversation starters (page 149) for some juicy questions. You'll also find some risqué shots on the next few pages to accompany your titillating tales.

Blow Job

2 parts Kahlúa
1 part Baileys Irish Cream

Layer in order and shoot.
Make this a Rattlesnake by adding Green Chartreuse.

Dirty Orgasm

½ oz (15 mL) Triple Sec liqueur
½ oz (15 mL) Galliano
½ oz (15 mL) Baileys Irish Cream

Layer in order.

Orgasm

⅔ oz (20mL) Baileys Irish Cream
⅔ oz (20mL) Cointreau

Build over ice. Garnish with strawberry or cherries.
A Multiple Orgasm is made with the addition of 1 oz
(30mL) of fresh cream or milk. A Screaming Multiple
Orgasm has the addition of ½ oz (15mL) Galliano along
with 1 oz (30mL) fresh cream or milk.

Sex in the Snow

⅓ oz (10mL) Triple sec, chilled
⅓ oz (10mL) Malibu rum, chilled
⅓ oz (10mL) ouzo, chilled

Pour in order, then stir. Shoot through a straw.

Hard On

⅔ oz (20mL) Kahlúa
½ oz (15mL) banana liqueur
⅓ oz (10mL) cream

Layer banana liqueur onto Kahlúa, then float the cream.

PREPARING YOUR NIGHT'S GOSSIP

IDLE TALK

Everyone likes a good gossip and sometimes it seems inevitable that conversation will turn this way. As the host, make sure that you always appear gracious and don't gossip too much in front of your guests. While gossiping can be fun, it can also be like Chinese whispers, and things that were said might look less funny or innocent the next day (especially if everyone's nursing a hangover).

Gossip about celebrities and pop culture can be more entertaining than gossiping about friends – the latest Hollywood romances, divorces and hairstyles is harmless fun and provides endless fodder for speculation. If you want to divert conversation from any 'nasty' gossip about someone who isn't present to defend themselves, try to bring up a trashy reality show, or an interesting actor or rock star instead.

Other topics for gossip might include new books, albums and TV shows, and what's hot or not in beauty, hair and fashion. A girls only event is also a great venue to show off new shoes, or to get out the clothes you used to wear 10 years ago for a laugh.

Remember, what you gossip about will often come back to bite. Maintain a 'do no harm' approach if you're gossiping about others.

PREPARING YOUR NIGHT'S POLE DANCING

SWINGING SISTERS

Pole dancing has become a popular fitness activity, keeping women strong and healthy as well as bringing some extra spice into their relationships. It's now offered at many gyms, as well as studios that focus exclusively on pole work.

Not everyone will be keen to try pole dancing, so make sure your guests are all on board before you spring it on them. Reiterate that the aim is to have some silly fun together, and maybe get a bit of exercise. If nobody is taking it too seriously, there's no reason for anyone to be embarrassed.

The easiest option will be to go to a venue that offers classes. You may well get a discount for a group, especially if you are first-time attendees. It's a popular activity for hen's parties, so studios sometimes offer packages with a lesson, cocktails and performances from experts.

Rather more difficult is installing your own pole. Generally they run from floor to ceiling, are made of steel or brass, and are affixed to the ceiling to ensure they stand sturdily. If you are a pole enthusiast, you might already have one in place, but make sure it won't pose a safety hazard for your guests before you all jump on and have a go! Alternatively you could arrange for a temporary pole to be brought in and installed.

An amazing work-out, as well as a fun and sexy activity, a girls' day out (or in) pole dancing can be a great bonding experience.

PREPARING YOUR NIGHT'S BELLY DANCING

ALLURING MOVES

Belly dancing parties are exotic fun for everyone. Depending on the country or music of origin, it can take many different forms. The Raqs Sharqi style, originally from Egypt, is the most familiar and is often performed at restaurants or cabaret shows.

It's possible to hire a teacher to come into your home or venue and give some lessons, as well as a performance. They sometimes bring a collection of scarves for guests to tie around their waist, made out of chiffon or cotton, with little coins attached to get those jingling sound affects. As with pole dancing, dance studios may offer food and drink packages with a belly dancing class, catering to hen's and birthday parties.

If you prefer to keep things DIY, you can easily obtain hip cloths yourself from stores selling harem clothing or second-hand shops. You might want to buy extra themed fabric to drape around the house and serve spicy nibbles and drinks to encourage the atmosphere of a Bedouin tent or Persian bazaar.

PREPARING YOUR NIGHT'S

INTERVENTION

DUMP THAT LOSER

WAKE-UP CALL

Supporting girlfriends who are obsessed with bad boys or losers is no easy task. We all have friends who are in love with someone that's not good for them or doesn't treat them as they deserve. We all know a girl who persists in an unhappy or dysfunctional relationship because she's afraid of being alone. And of course, we all have that friend who is mysteriously obsessed with a 'meh' guy who shows zero interest in her.

Most of the time, we're happy to indulge our girlfriends about these useless boys and going-nowhere relationships (and hope they'll indulge us when we're in the same boat). We listen to the stories over and over: he didn't call, he didn't show up, he let me down, I think he's sleeping with someone else. We offer what advice we can and hope things will change for the better. But sometimes they don't, and things reach such a boiling point that intervention seems the only option.

Warning: this is a last resort! Staging an intervention is very difficult to pull off without royally embarrassing and irritating your friend. Your aim should be to show her your support, while also communicating that she is wasting her best years on this creep and that nobody in their right mind could think he is the right guy for her. This is obviously an awkward thing to explain with sensitivity. If possible, everyone should give reasonable examples of Mr Wrong's dreadful behaviour. Try, if you can, to avoid coming across as condescending.

Interventions of this kind can be very cleansing if done right. I've been to one where we all brought photos of the guy, put them in a garbage bin and set them on fire.

It's probably a good idea to do this outside, near a hose. Then maybe have a long break for beverages.

Sperm Shooter

½ oz (15mL) banana liqueur
½ oz (15mL) fresh cream (chilled)

Pour ingredients into a shot glass, stir and serve

G Spot

½ oz (15mL) Champord raspberry liqueur
½ oz (15mL) Southern Comfort
½ oz (15mL) fresh orange juice

Pour ingredients into a cocktail shaker over ice and shake. Strain into a chilled shot glass and serve.

Kick Him In The Balls

Glass: 5 oz (140mL) Champagne saucer

1 oz (30mL) rum
1 oz (30mL) orange juice
1 oz (30mL) melon liqueur
1 oz (30mL) cream
½ oz (15mL) coconut cream
Melon balls soaked in Corbua rum

Shake with ice and strain.
Float with two melon balls that have been marinated in Coruba Rum and refrigerated. Using a toothpick, eat both balls together and you'll be sure to feel that 'Kick in the Balls'.

Off The Leash

Glass: 5 oz (140mL) Champagne saucer

3 oz (90mL) brandy
1 oz (30mL) sweet vermouth
Cracked ice
3 maraschino cherries for garnish

Mix all ingredients in a mixing glass and strain into Champagne saucer. Garnish with maraschino cherries and serve.

PREPARING YOUR NIGHT'S DIVORCE CELEBRATION

SPLITASTIC

Divorce doesn't have to be just a sad, emotional and exhausting experience. It's also a time of release, freedom and new beginnings. So why not celebrate with a divorce party?

As long as the freshly-minted divorcée is into it (obviously) this can be a lot of fun. There will likely be a good deal of drinking; try some of the shots and cocktails throughout this book. You might like to watch some classic movies about women making good after a marriage break-up – think 'Eat Pray Love'. Dancing to a cheesy yet inspiring playlist, with songs like 'I Will Survive' and 'I Am Woman' on heavy rotation, can do wonders.

Divorce parties are also likely to involve discussion of the ex and the fantasy revenge you'd like to carry out on him. Sticking an entire fish under his bed, which he won't find until the smell has really set in, or leaving a carton of milk in his hot car. You may find that setting up a dartboard with his face pinned to it, or whacking an ex-shaped piñata, can be very satisfying.

Just remember that while you may have said all along you didn't like him, your friend once did – enough to marry him. Even a happy divorce can be a sensitive thing, so take care not to hurt or offend the guest of honour.

PREPARING YOUR BABY SHOWER

BUN IN THE OVEN

Baby showers come in all different styles, from silly and light-hearted to elegant and refined. Usually friends, family and co-workers attend and these days men will often make the invite list, too. The shower is typically hosted by a close friend rather then a relative.

There are no hard and fast rules about how many guests should be invited and what the entertainment should be, but do check with the mum-to-be if she doesn't want any games, a tradition at baby showers. The most popular game is to guess the baby's birth date, gender and sometimes the weight. Other games might include bobbing for rubber duckies, quizzes about celebrity children or mums and estimating the diameter of the belly.

If it is a gift-giving party, you need to be prepared to field lots of questions about what the mother wants. Typical gifts are generic clothes if you don't know the sex, toys that are baby-safe and tested by the manufacturer, diapers (always welcome) and baby bottles. If your guests want to put in for a larger gift, you should check with someone close to the showeree whether they have already purchased the item. To ease all this confusion, it might be better to sign up for a gift registry.

Every culture has its own baby shower customs, but typically it occurs one month to six weeks before the baby is due.

The next pages feature gorgeous mocktails that everyone, including the mother-to-be, can enjoy.

Mockatini

Glass: 3 oz (90mL) cocktail glass

½ oz (15mL) lime juice
Dash of lemon juice
2 oz (60mL) tonic water
1 green olive

Stir liquid ingredients with ice and strain. Garnish with a green olive on a toothpick or a lemon twist.

Blunt Screwdriver

Glass: 9½ oz (285mL) highball glass

4 oz (120mL) ginger ale
4 oz (120mL) orange juice
Slice of orange
1 red cherry

Build over ice. Garnish with the orange slice and red cherry.
Note: This cousin of the well-known alcoholic Screwdriver substitutes ginger ale for vodka. Add
½ oz (15mL) grenadine for a Roy Rogers.

Alice in Wonderland

Glass: 6 oz (180mL) tulip cocktail glass

3½ oz (100mL) grapefruit juice
1 oz (30mL) green tea
2/3 oz (20mL) lemon juice
½ oz (15mL) sugar syrup
Soda water
1 grape

Build over ice and top up with soda water. Garnish with a grape.

Cranberry Zinger

Glass: 9½ oz (285mL) footed highball glass

4 oz (120mL) cranberry juice
2 tsps brown sugar
1 tsp lemon extract
1 cup pineapple pieces
8 oz (250mL) ginger ale

Combine all ingredients except ginger ale. Add ginger ale and ice before serving.

Virgin Mary

Glass: 9½ oz (285mL) fancy cocktail glass
150mL tomato juice
½ oz (15mL) lemon juice
1 tsp Worcestershire sauce
Dash of Tabasco
Salt and pepper
1 stalk celery
1 stick cucumber
Slice of lemon

Blend tomato juice, lemon juice, Worcestershire sauce, Tabasco, salt and pepper together. Serve with ice, garnished with celery stalk, cucumber stick and slice of lemon.

Shirley Temple

Glass: 9½ oz (285mL) highball glass

½ oz (15mL) grenadine
10 oz (270mL) ginger ale or lemonade
Slice of orange

Build over ice. Garnish with the slice of orange and serve. Note: For a tangy variation, try a Shirley Temple No.2. Add 2 oz (60mL) pineapple juice to a glass half-full of ice. Top with lemonade, float ½ oz (15mL) passionfruit pulp on top, garnish with a pineapple wedge and cherry.

PREPARING YOUR HEN'S NIGHT

BRIDAL PARTY

Every bride-to-be – or shall we call her the bachelorette? – should have some sort of celebration to mark her memorable change in relationship status from single girl to married woman. And what better way to do that than a hen's night?

If you are planning a hen's, then the bride is probably a close friend or relative, and her personal taste should inform the whole event – just as you'd hope she would consider your taste if your positions were reversed. If she's a wild child, she might like a night out on the tiles, but if she's a bit more reserved, that could be her worst nightmare (although they do say it's the quiet ones you have to watch). If in doubt, consult other friends and family, or the bride herself. It's good etiquette to send invitations as early as possible and stipulate an RSVP date. Spell out what you're planning to do and the costs involved so your guests won't be surprised.

There are loads of options for activities. Weekends away are becoming more popular, with winery tours, spa resorts and other glamorous destinations (Las Vegas, anyone?) on the cards. But something simpler, shorter or closer to home might be preferable, in which case cooking or cocktail-making classes, a pampering session, or drinks and dancing till the wee hours are all possibilities.

Going out for a long, delicious dinner is great. You might ask the restaurant if you can decorate the table with balloons and photos of the bride, or even put together a personalised menu sheet with some fun facts about her. They may offer deals if you are a big group. Race days are also really fun and a nice way to class up the event, with everyone in their most fabulous dresses, heels and hats. Just remember it's a long day; if drinking Champagne, keep the water flowing between glasses, and don't forget to wear sunscreen.

No matter the venue, you will need to consider hiring a limo or bus to move everyone around together. Food is also important when alcohol is involved so plan on lunch or dinner breaks and take snacks if you can.

Bridezilla

Glass: 5 oz (140mL) Cocktail glass

½ oz (15mL) dry vermouth
3 dashes strawberry liqueur
½ oz (15mL) gin
4 strawberries, leaves removed
½ (15mL) sweet vermouth (rosso or bianco)
4 ice cubes

Blend two ice cubes, gin, both types of vermouth, strawberry liqueur and two strawberries.
Pour into glass over remaining ice cubes.
Garnish with remaining strawberries to serve.

Blushing Bride

Glass: 5 oz (140mL) Champagne saucer

1 oz (30mL) peach schnapps
1 oz (30mL) grenadine
4 oz (120mL) Champagne

Pour the peach schnapps and grenadine into a Champagne flute.
Top with Champagne.

PREPARING YOUR KITCHEN TEA

THE REFINED HEN'S

The kitchen tea is a quieter, more casual event for the bride-to-be. It's about cultivating a relaxed atmosphere in which everyone can chat and offer advice. Typically it would be suitable for the bride's mum or gran to attend.

Some people like to book companies to come in and sell products, such as homewares, which the guests can purchase for the bride. Others do a cellar party, where the host asks each guest to bring a bottle of spirits, Champagne or wine as a gift for the bridge and groom.

Some kitchen teas get wilder than the name might suggest, involving sex toy parties or lingerie events. If you're ordering a stripper, make sure the bride hasn't invited any frail or stuffy relatives, especially in-laws, as this might not sit too well with them! Check first with a relative or another close friend.

Don't forget to think about whether the guests will bring their own beverages or if you will need to provide them. Food is also important to think about. Are you providing easy nibbles and biscuits, like those described in the following pages, or a full high tea menu? An easy method is to ask your guests to bring along a plate, which means the bridal party won't be left with a massive bill.

Kitchen teas usually only run for 2–4 hours. These events may well be attended by children, so make sure your home or the venue is child-friendly and you have a dedicated space for children.

Traditional Shortbread

Makes 25 • Preparation 10 minutes • Cooking 30 minutes

8 oz (250g) butter, at room temperature
1 cup icing (confectioners') sugar
1 cup cornflour
1 cup plain (all-purpose) flour

Preheat oven to 300°F (150°C). Lightly butter a baking tray.

Cream butter and icing sugar until light and fluffy. Sift cornflour and flour together. Mix sifted ingredients into creamed mixture, and knead well.

Roll out between two sheets of baking paper to 1cm thickness. Cut into 1¼ x 2¾in (3 x 7cm) fingers, then place on the baking tray. Prick around the edges with a fork.

Bake for 30 minutes or until pale golden.

Florentines

Makes 20 • Preparation 25 minutes • Cooking 10 minutes

4 oz (125g) butter, at room temperature
½ cup sugar
5 tbsps golden syrup
¼ cup plain (all-purpose) flour
1 cup sliced almonds
½ cup glacé cherries, chopped
½ cup walnuts, chopped
¼ cup mixed peel, chopped
5 oz (150g) cooking chocolate

Preheat oven to 350°F (180°C). Line 4 oven trays with baking paper.

Cream butter and sugar, then beat in golden syrup. Sift in flour, add almonds, cherries, walnuts and peel and mix well. Place tablespoonfuls of mixture onto a tray, leaving plenty of room for the cookies to spread. Using a knife, press each one out as flat and round as possible. Cook no more than 4 or 5 to a tray.

Bake for 10 minutes or until golden brown. Remove from oven and leave on tray for 5 minutes before transferring to a wire rack.

Meanwhile, melt chocolate in a bowl over simmering water. When the biscuits are cold, ice with chocolate on their flat sides.

Chocolate Peanut Cookies

Makes 25 • Preparation 20 minutes • Cooking 15 minutes

¾ cup plain (all-purpose) flour
¼ tsp baking powder
½ tsp salt
4 oz (125g) unsalted butter, at room temperature
¾ cup brown sugar
2 tbsps caster sugar
1 vanilla pod, split in half lengthwise
1 egg
3 tsps milk
1 cup rolled oats
1 cup unsalted peanuts
1 heaped cup dark chocolate chips

Preheat oven to 325°F (160°C). Line two baking trays with baking paper.

Combine flour, baking powder and salt in a bowl.

Beat the butter, brown sugar, caster sugar and seeds from vanilla pod in an electric mixer until the mixture has become thick and pale. Add the egg and milk, then beat in the flour mixture with the rolled oats. Fold in the peanuts and chocolate.

Drop tablespoonfuls of the dough onto the baking trays. Bake for 15 minutes, then remove from the oven and allow to cool on a wire rack.

Chocolate Pecan Fingers

Makes about 15 fingers

3 oz (90g) dark chocolate
4 oz (125g) butter
2 tsps instant coffee powder
2 eggs
¾ cup superfine (caster) sugar
½ tsp vanilla
½ cup all-purpose (plain) flour
¾ cup pecans, chopped
Icing (confectioners') sugar

Melt the chocolate and butter together over hot water, stir in the coffee powder and allow to cool slightly.

In a medium-sized bowl whisk the eggs until foamy and add the sugar and vanilla. Fold the chocolate mixture through the eggs. Stir in the flour and pecans and mix until just blended.

Spoon the mixture into a lightly greased 8in (20cm) square cake pan. Bake at 350°F (180°C) for 25 minutes or until cake springs back when touched. Cool in the tin. Dust with sifted icing sugar and cut into fingers to serve.

Caramel Squares

Makes 24

SHORTBREAD BASE:
3½ oz (100g) butter
3 tbsps sugar
2 oz (60g) cornflour, sifted
¾ cup plain (all-purpose) flour, sifted

CARAMEL FILLING:
4 oz (125g) butter
½ cup brown sugar
2 tbsps honey
14 oz (400g) sweetened condensed milk
1 tsp vanilla extract
Chocolate topping
7 oz (200g) dark chocolate, melted

Preheat oven to 350°F (180°C).

To make base, place butter and sugar in a bowl and beat until light and fluffy. Mix in cornflour and flour, turn onto a lightly floured surface and knead briefly, then press into a buttered and lined 8 x 12in (20 x 30cm) shallow cake tin and bake for 25 minutes or until firm.

To make filling, place butter, brown sugar and honey in a saucepan and cook over a medium heat, stirring constantly until sugar melts and ingredients are combined. Bring to the boil and simmer for 7 minutes. Beat in condensed milk and vanilla extract, pour filling over base and bake for 20 minutes longer. Set aside to cool completely.

Spread melted chocolate over filling, set aside until firm, then cut into squares.

Creamy Chocolate Cheesecake

Serves 8

BASE:
3½ oz (100g) low-fat digestive biscuits
2 oz (55g) butter
1 tbsp golden syrup

FILLING:
7 oz (200g) cream cheese
2 tbsps caster (superfine) sugar
3½ oz (100g) semisweet chocolate drops
1 oz (30 g) cocoa powder, sifted
1 cup thickened cream
1 oz (30 g) semisweet chocolate, shaved

Preheat the oven to 350°F (180°C).

For the base, put the biscuits into a plastic bag and crush with a rolling pin. Gently heat the butter and golden syrup until melted, stirring. Mix in the biscuits, then pack into an 18cm (7in) loose-bottomed cake tin and cook for 15 minutes or until crisp. Cool for 20 minutes.

For the filling, beat the cream cheese with the sugar until soft. Melt half the chocolate drops in a bowl set over a saucepan of simmering water. Blend the cocoa to a paste with 2 tablespoons of boiling water. Stir into the melted chocolate and then fold in the cream cheese mixture. Stir in the remaining chocolate drops.

Whip half of the cream until it forms soft peaks. Fold it into the chocolate mixture, then spoon over the biscuit base. Refrigerate for 2 hours or until set. Remove from the tin. Whip the remaining cream and spread over the cheesecake and top with the chocolate shavings.

Note: To make this cheesecake even more decadent, beat a little fruity liqueur into the cream.

PREPARING YOUR PAMPER NIGHT

TREAT YOURSELF

The green tea is steeping and the zen music is playing gently in the background. It's time for you to get out the foot lotions and facial creams for a girls' night of pampering. This event is all about relaxation, indulgence and hanging out with your girlfriends.

An easy way to set up a pamper night is to ask a local beauty therapist to come along and do facials, manicures and pedicures. Alternatively, guests could each buy some lotions, treatments or nail polishes. Then you can share the goodies to do each other's nails, facials and even hairstyles.

Another idea is to bring in a professional to do massages. Just make sure you have set aside a quiet, private space for this.

Juices and smoothies are essential for a relaxation night, as is light, healthy food. Provide lots of fruits and raw vegetables and keep the chilled water and herbal tea flowing. Warm face-towels are a lovely indulgence and guests should come in their most comfortable clothes, or even in robes or PJs. All this combined with the great company of your friends is sure to make for an amazing night in.

PREPARING YOUR GIRLS' NIGHT IN

HOME TO ROOST

If you're planning a simple night in with the girls, and have no theme or style in mind, still make a plan for what you will be doing. You don't want to end up bored in front of the TV if you can help it. Even just making some cocktails, finger food or tapas can lend a quiet night in that special something. If you don't want to cook, put out some cheese and biscuits or order take-out.

Also ensure you have the space ready for where you plan to hold your night. Have everything you want prepared and to hand – for example, if you're going to be watching movies, have the TV and DVD player all set up, along with plenty of blankets and cushions.

Be sure to lock away any items you don't want your friends to find, like pictures of you from school that remind you of how dorky you were back then.

PREPARING YOUR HIGH TEA

LADIES AT TABLE

High tea is now one of the most popular events you can do and is suitable for celebrating most occasions. It is typically held in the late morning or afternoon, and consists of small meals and lots of yummy cakes.

The term 'high tea' was used as far back as 1825. 'High' suggests luxury ingredients, from fresh salmon to beautiful jams, as well as food that is rich in calories and fat, containing (and served with) lots of real butter.

Preparing your high tea can be as simple as running out and purchasing traditional scones, cakes and biscuits from your local gourmet bakeries and delis, but if you're feeling domestic, you can make them yourself the night before. We've supplied a bunch of great recipes in the following pages. Prepare sandwiches on the day, at most a few hours beforehand. Popular choices are smoked salmon, cucumber and egg and cress; you'll find some recipes for these here, too.

Don't forget cloth napkins (linen or cotton), pretty crockery and serving dishes, and think about your décor and table decorations. Ensure that you have enough spoons and forks for all your guests.

Obviously tea is traditionally served, so having a teapot is ideal, china or silver-plated. You can often pick these up at vintage and second-hand shops. Some high teas also serve Champagne and orange juice.

If you decide to host a high tea, don't forget it's about grace and elegance, so make sure your event has a touch of class.

Lavender Tea

2-3 sprigs lavender
3 thin slices of ginger root
1 tsp of honey
3 cardamom pods

Take 2–3 sprigs (or enough to fill one-quarter of a cup) of lavender. Pour 1 cup of boiling water over this, and add ginger root, honey and cardamom pods. Crush well with a spoon. Stand for 5 minutes, strain and sip slowly, preferably while lying in a bath made fragrant with fresh lavender hung under the tap, lavender soap and bath oil and a lavender-scented candle. Relax.

Raspberry Iced Tea

1 large raspberry leaf
18 fruits
1 stick of cinnamon
2 cloves
1 tsp of lemon zest
2 slices of cucumber
Sprig of fresh mint

Take the large raspberry leaf with 6 fruits, cinnamon and cloves. Pour over this 1 cup of boiling water, add lemon zest and stir well. Stand for 5 minutes. Strain and cool. Now add 12 more raspberries and cucumber and fresh mint. Whirl in a liquidiser. Add ice, serve chilled. It's refreshingly unusual and delicious! You can also add honey if liked.

Bergamot Earl Grey Spicy Tea

1 Earl Grey tea bag
2 bergamot leaves
1 cinnamon stick
1 lemon slice
Cinnamon powder
1 fresh lemon slice
Honey to taste

Pour 1 cup of boiling water over the tea bag and 2 bergamot leaves, 1 cinnamon stick and 1 lemon slice. Remove the tea bag after 10–15 seconds. Stand for 5 minutes and stir frequently with the cinnamon stick. Strain, pour into a pretty mug, and add a sprinkling of cinnamon powder, a fresh lemon slice and a touch of honey.

Dainty Shrimp/Prawn Circles

Makes 15

2 tbsps mayonnaise
2 tsps tomato sauce
A dash of Worcestershire sauce
Salt and black pepper
6½ oz (200g) fresh peeled cooked shrimp/prawns (roughly chopped, depending on the size)
10 slices of soft white sliced fresh bread, lightly buttered
½ tsp paprika
Watercress or mustard cress, to garnish

Combine mayonnaise, tomato sauce and Worcestershire sauce. Season with salt and pepper. This mixture must be quite stiff, otherwise it will not coat the shrimp/prawns and will make a soggy sandwich.

Add shrimp/prawns and stir gently to coat.

Cut three circles out of each slice of bread using a 1½in (4cm) cookie cutter (serrated is best for a pretty edge). Spread 2 teaspoons shrimp/prawn mixture onto 15 circles. Sprinkle each with paprika. Top with remaining fresh bread circles.

Arrange on a large platter, garnished with watercress or mustard cress.

Smoked Salmon, Dill and Cucumber

Makes 6 dainty sandwiches

1 tbsp whole egg mayonnaise
2 tsps baby capers, chopped
1 tsp chopped fresh dill
4 slices soft white fresh bread, lightly buttered
1½–3½ oz (50–100g) smoked salmon (or smoked trout)
¼ small or English cucumber, finely sliced
Black pepper

Combine the mayonnaise, chopped capers and dill and spread on the two slices of fresh bread. Place the smoked salmon generously on top. Overlap nine thin slices of cucumber until it is covering the salmon. Season with freshly ground black pepper.

Top with second slice of fresh bread. Trim crusts off sandwich and cut into three fingers, then cut each finger in half.

Crab, Chives and Celery

You can buy fresh crabmeat from good supermarkets and delicatessens. Frozen or tinned can also be used.

Makes 6 dainty fingers

¼ stick celery, very finely chopped
½ tbsp crème fraiche
2 garlic chives (or ordinary chives), finely chopped
2½ oz (70g) crabmeat
Salt and black pepper
4 slices soft white bread, lightly buttered

Mix the celery with the crème fraiche and chives. Add the crabmeat, gently stirring to combine. Season well with salt and pepper.

Spread the mixture onto two slices of fresh bread. Top with second slice of bread. Trim the crusts and cut into three fingers, then cut each finger in half.

Chicken and Walnut

Chicken is such a versatile ingredient, perfect for sandwiches. The texture and taste of shredded chicken breast is quite distinct and subtle.

Makes 6 dainty fingers

½ tbsp cream cheese (softened)
½ tbsp mayonnaise
1 tbsp milk
A handful of walnuts, finely chopped
½ poached chicken breast (approx. 3½ oz, or 100g), shredded
1 tbsp flat-leaf parsley, chopped
Salt and black pepper
4 slices soft wholemeal fresh bread, lightly buttered

Mix the cream cheese and mayonnaise together. If a more liquid consistency is needed to coat the chicken, add a small quantity of milk.

Stir the walnuts into the mayonnaise mixture. Add the shredded chicken and chopped parsley, and mix to combine. Season to taste.

Divide the mixture onto two slices of fresh bread and top with the other slices. Trim crusts off sandwich and cut into three fingers, then cut each finger in half.

Malted Milk Mini Cupcakes

Makes 24

2½ oz (80g) butter, softened
½ cup caster (superfine) sugar
1 egg
1 tbsp cocoa powder, sifted
1 cup self-raising flour, sifted
¹/₃ cup milk
½ tsp vanilla extract

TOPPING:
2½ oz (80g) butter, softened
1 cup icing (confectioners') sugar
2 tbsps malted milk powder
24 chocolate covered malt balls

Preheat the oven to 325°F (160°C). Line a 24 mini cupcake pan with mini cupcake papers. In a medium-sized bowl, use an electric mixer on high speed to cream the butter and sugar until light and fluffy. Add the egg and mix well.

Add the cocoa, flour, milk and vanilla, and beat with an electric mixer on medium until well combined.

Divide the mixture evenly between the 24 mini cupcake papers. Bake for 10 – 15 minutes until well risen and firm to the touch. Allow to cool for a few minutes, then transfer to a wire rack. Allow to cool fully before icing.

For the topping, use an electric mixer on high speed to beat the butter and malted milk powder, until light and fluffy. Gradually beat in icing sugar until all combined, continue beating for 1 minute. Place mixture into a piping bag with a plain nozzle and pipe onto cupcakes. Decorate with chocolate malt balls.

Cheesecake with Strawberries

BASE:
6 oz (175g) butter
12 oz (350g) biscuit crumbs

FILLING:
2 oz (60g) brown sugar
8 oz (250g) cream cheese, softened
3 eggs, lightly beaten
1 cup sugar
1 tsp lemon juice
2 tsps vanilla extract
2 cups sour cream
1/2 cup fresh strawberries

Preheat oven to 325°F (160°C).

For base, melt butter in saucepan over medium heat. Stir in crumbs and sugar. Take a 10in (25cm) springform tin and pack the mixture into the sides and bottom to make a base. Bake for 10 minutes.

For the filling, beat cream cheese, eggs, sugar, lemon juice and vanilla together well, then mix in sour cream. Pour over crust, raise oven temperature to 350°F (180°C) and bake for 1 hour.

Let stand at least 2 hours. Chill until required. Use fresh strawberries to top the cheesecake.

Mini Strawberry Custard Tarts

Makes 12

12 frozen mini shortcrust pastry cases
2 egg yolks
2 tbsps caster (superfine) sugar
1/3 cup thickened cream
1½ tbsps strawberry jam
6 small strawberries, hulled and halved
1 tbsp icing sugar

Preheat the oven to 325°F (160°C). Place the frozen tart cases on an oven tray and bake for 10 minutes. Remove from the oven and set aside to cool slightly.

Meanwhile, whisk the egg yolks and sugar by hand until the sugar dissolves, then stir in the cream. Spread the base of each tart case with half a teaspoon of strawberry jam. Spoon the egg mixture evenly into each tart case, then bake for 10–12 minutes until the custard is set. When set, take from the oven and place a strawberry half, cut-side down, onto each tart.

Leave to cool for 15 minutes, then remove the foil cases. Place on a platter and dust with icing sugar to serve.

Traditional Scones

Makes 12

2 cups self-raising flour
1 tsp baking powder
2 tsps sugar
1½ oz (45g) butter
1 egg
½ cup milk

Preheat oven to 425°F (220°C).

Sift flour and baking powder into a large bowl. Stir in sugar, then rub in butter using fingertips until mixture resembles coarse breadcrumbs.

Whisk together egg and milk. Make a well in centre of flour mixture, pour in egg mixture and mix to form a soft dough. Turn onto a lightly floured surface and knead lightly.

Press dough out to a 1in (25mm) thickness using the palm of your hand. Cut out scones using a floured 2in (5cm) cutter. Avoid twisting the cutter, or the scones will rise unevenly.

Arrange scones close together on a buttered and lightly floured baking tray or in a shallow 8in (20cm) round cake tin. Brush with a little milk and bake for 12–15 minutes or until golden.

Butterscotch Buns

Makes 12

2 oz (60g) butter, softened, plus 1½ oz (45g) chilled
¾ cup brown sugar, packed
2 cups plain (all-purpose) flour
2 tbsps granulated sugar
4 tsps baking powder
1 tsp salt
¾ cup milk
⅓ cup chopped nuts

Preheat oven to 430°F (220°C). Cream softened butter and brown sugar together in a small bowl. Set aside.

In a large bowl, combine flour, sugar, baking powder and salt. Cut in chilled butter until crumbly. Make a well in the centre.

Pour milk into the well. Stir to make a soft dough. Knead 8–10 times. Pat or roll out on lightly floured surface to 9–10 in (23–25cm) square. Spread with brown sugar mixture.

Sprinkle with nuts. Roll up as for jelly roll. Pinch edge to seal. Cut into 12 slices. Place on buttered 8 x 8in (20 x 20cm) pan. Bake 15–20 minutes. Invert over tray while hot.

Hazelnut Shortbreads

Makes 40

8 oz (250g) butter, chopped
1½ cups plain (all-purpose) flour, sifted
1½ oz (45g) hazelnuts, ground
¼ cup ground rice
¼ cup caster (superfine) sugar
3½ oz (100g) chocolate, melted

Preheat oven to 325°F(160°C).

Place butter, flour, hazelnuts and ground rice in a food processor and process until mixture resembles coarse breadcrumbs. Add sugar and process to combine.

Turn mixture onto a floured surface and knead lightly to make a pliable dough. Place dough between sheets of baking paper and roll out to ¼in (5mm) thick. Using a 2in (5cm) fluted cutter, cut out rounds of dough and place 1in (25mm) apart on buttered baking trays. Bake for 20–25 minutes or until lightly browned. Stand on baking trays for 2–3 minutes before transferring to wire racks to cool.

Place melted chocolate in a plastic food bag, snip off one corner and pipe lines across each biscuit before serving.

Mascarpone and Fruit Tartlets

Makes 24

2 sheets frozen shortcrust pastry, thawed
8 oz (250 g) soft mascarpone
6½ oz (200 g) blueberries, picked over
6½ oz (200 g) strawberries, hulls removed, sliced
2 tbsps icing (confectioner's) sugar, sifted

Preheat oven to 375°F (190°C). Place pastry on work surface and cut 24 rounds using a 2½in (6cm) cookie cutter. Line greased mini muffin pans with pastry rounds. Bake until golden, about 12 minutes. Remove pans from oven and turn pastry cups onto a wire rack and allow to cool.

In a small bowl, beat mascarpone with a wooden spoon until smooth and pliable. Spoon 2 teaspoons mascarpone into each cup.

Arrange berries attractively over mascarpone and dust with sugar just before serving.

Coffeetines

Makes 24 • Preparation 15 minutes • Cooking 10 minutes

½ cup thickened cream
½ cup caster (superfine) sugar
1 cup hazelnuts, finely chopped
3½ oz (100g) candied orange peel, finely chopped
2 tsps instant coffee
¼ cup plain flour
7 oz (200g) chocolate
¼ tsp vegetable oil
2 tbsps strong
Espresso coffee

Preheat oven to 170°C.

Mix together the cream, sugar, nuts, peel, instant coffee and flour to form a dough. Drop 1 teaspoonful at a time onto baking paper, approximately 1½ in (4cm) apart. Flatten with a knife dipped in cold water.

Bake for 10 minutes, or until browned around the edges. Cool, flat-side up, on racks.

Once completely cool, combine the chocolate, oil and espresso in a bowl and microwave until chocolate only just begins to melt, stirring every 20 seconds – be careful not to burn the chocolate. Spread chocolate over the flat side of each biscuit.

Hazelchocs

Makes 16 • Preparation 20 minutes • Cooking 20 minutes

4 oz (120g) butter
4 tbsps caster (superfine) sugar
4 tbsps brown sugar
1 cup plain (all-purpose) flour
3 tbsps rice flour
2 tbsps cornflour
2 tbsps instant coffee, plus 1 tsp
2 tbsps milk
3 tbsps hazelnuts, toasted and finely chopped
½ cup chocolate hazelnut spread
3½ oz (100g) dark cooking chocolate, melted

Preheat oven to 340°F (170°C). Lightly butter 2 baking trays.

Beat butter and sugars in a small bowl with an electric mixer until pale and fluffy. Stir in sifted flours and 2 tablespoons of the coffee in two batches, then stir in milk and nuts.

Roll tablespoonfuls into balls and flatten slightly. Place 1¼in (3cm) apart on the baking trays. Bake for about 20 minutes or until pale golden. Cool on a wire rack.

Meanwhile, combine hazelnut spread and chocolate in a bowl. Refrigerate, stirring often, until spreadable.

Join 2 biscuits with 1–2 teaspoons of hazelnut chocolate. Repeat with remaining biscuits.

PREPARING YOUR HANGOVER CURES

QUICK FIXES FOR SORE HEADS

After a spectacular girls only event, you've woken up with the hangover from hell – pain, fuzziness, dizziness, parched mouth and that feeling like you're going to need to make camp near the bathroom.

If you didn't drink water before bed, it's worth starting with a glass or two now. Don't forget to suggest this to your guests as they leave your party or event. Green tea is the ideal hot beverage for hangovers, so it could be fun to give out little gift bags with a green-tea bag enclosed. It should be noted that while most us reach for coffee, it's actually a diuretic, and not always helpful when you're hungover.

Honey can help too. This sweet, sticky spread provides you with sodium, and makes for a healthy pick-me-up on wholemeal toast. Another food to consider is cabbage. It is rich in folic acid, which is vital for energy and plays an important role in the production of red blood cells. Salty foods can also help release energy slowly, so a bacon sandwich on brown bread will go down perfectly. Juices packed with fruit and vegetables, especially those high in Vitamin C, are also refreshing the morning after.

But if you're eating healthy most the time, why not use this as an excuse for a fry-up? A hot breakfast full of saturated fats can be just the ticket. And a brutal hangover is the best excuse to indulge in a classic breakfast of bacon and eggs without feeling too guilty. The well prepared will have everything they need for a morning after breakfast already on hand, so there is no need to run to the supermarket when feeling terrible.

While I'm not a big believer that one should drink alcohol the day after a heavy night, I have seen my friends indulge in the 'hair of the dog' and feel better within an hour. This is a highly debatable cure and there is a danger of excessive consumption of alcohol, so it might not be the wisest choice.

Bloody Mary

1½ oz (45mL) vodka
1½ tsps lemon juice
2 drops Worcestershire sauce
2 drops Tabasco
Salt and pepper to taste
Tomato juice
Celery stick to garnish

Combine liquid ingredients over ice in a highball or Collins glass and stir well. Garnish with celery stick, olive, marinated string bean or vegetable of choice. Serve with swizzle stick and straw.

Mini Burgers

Everyone is serving mini burgers at parties these days, as they provide a handy meal in the hand, but they are also brilliant for a hangover. The mini 'bake at home' rolls from the supermarket provide the perfect size and torpedo shape to hold the ingredients.

Makes 8

1 small onion, very finely chopped
8 oz (250g) beef mince
2 beef stock cubes
Salt and pepper
8 mini baguettes/rolls
1 tbsp tomato sauce
8 small lettuce leaves, plus extra for garnish
4 cherry tomatoes, sliced into 4
8 baby beetroot slices (optional)
1 tbsp mayonnaise
5–6 cornichons, sliced thinly (optional)

Gently cook the onions until soft, then allow to cool. Combine mince, cooled onions and crumbled (dry) stock cubes and mix together well. Season with salt and pepper.

Divide the mixture into 8 and roll each portion into a ball. Squash slightly to flatten into a burger or sausage shape (depending on the shape of the bread roll you are using). Shallow fry (or grill) the burgers for approximately 4 minutes on each side, ensuring that they are browned on the outside and cooked through.

If using cook-at-home rolls, bake them in the oven according to the packet instructions. Split the rolls in half, keeping the halves attached, and spread the tomato sauce on one side.

Put the cooked burgers inside the rolls. Layer the lettuce, tomato, beetroot and top with a blob of mayonnaise and a few slices of cornichon.

Serve on a large platter garnished with mini lettuce leaves.

BLT

Makes 2 sandwiches

4 rashers short (middle) bacon
4 slices wholemeal or white bread, from a square loaf
1 tbsp aioli
2 tomatoes, sliced
¼ iceberg lettuce, shredded
Salt and black pepper
Mixed leaves, to garnish
Tomato wedges, to garnish

Cook the bacon in a frying pan or grill, blot with kitchen paper to remove excess fat.

Toast the fresh bread lightly and spread each slice with the aioli (for extra punch, rub a cut, raw garlic clove over the toast).

Place bacon, tomato slices and shredded lettuce, in that order, on the aioli.

Season with salt and pepper. Top with second slice of toast. Cut in half on the diagonal and serve with a side of dressed mixed leaves and tomato wedges.

Butternut Pancakes

2½ oz (75g) butternut squash
1 egg, separated
1 tbsp safflower oil (or othervegetable oil)
1 cup milk or soymilk
¼ cup apple sauce
1½ cups wholewheat pastry flour
¼ tsp sea salt
½ tsp cinnamon
1½ tsps baking powder
Maple syrup and seasonal fruit

Cut the butternut squash into large cubes and steam for 5 minutes until soft, then cool.

Beat egg white until stiff. In a separate bowl, beat egg yolk, oil, butternut squash, milk and apple sauce.

In another bowl, sift the remaining dry ingredients, then stir in the butternut mixture. Gently fold in the egg white.

Lightly oil a large frying pan and heat. Test by sprinkling a few drops of water – if it bubbles, the heat is right. For each pancake, pour approximately 3–4 tablespoonfuls of batter into the pan. When bubbles appear on top of the pancakes, turn and cook until the other side has just become brown.

Serve with real maple syrup and fresh seasonal fruit.

French Toast

4 eggs
½ cup milk
1 oz (30g) butter
8 slices raisin or fruit bread
Maple syrup and fruit

Whisk together eggs and milk in a large shallow dish. Place bread slices in egg mixture and coat well on both sides.

Heat the butter in a non-stick frying pan over low to medium heat. Cook bread for about 1–2 minutes each side or until golden.

Cut bread in half and serve with sliced banana (or other fresh or canned fruit) and maple syrup.

Mixed Mushrooms on Herbed Muffins

Serves 6

12 oz (350g) mixed mushrooms, including wild, oyster and shiitake
2 tbsps olive oil
Salt and freshly ground black pepper
$^2/_3$ oz (20g) butter
1 clove garlic, crushed
¼ cup fresh parsley, chopped
½ small bunch chives, chopped
2 tsps sherry vinegar or balsamic vinegar
1½ oz (40g) low-fat soft cheese
2 English muffins

Halve any large mushrooms. Heat 2 teaspoons of the oil in a heavy-based frying pan, then add the mushrooms. Season lightly and fry over a medium to high heat for 5 minutes or until they start to release their juices.

Remove the mushrooms and drain on absorbent paper, then set aside. Add the rest of the oil and half the butter to the pan and heat until the butter melts. Add the garlic and stir for 1 minute.

Return the mushrooms to the pan, then increase the heat to high and fry for 5 minutes or until they are tender and starting to crisp. Stir in the remaining butter and 1 tablespoon each of parsley and chives, drizzle with the vinegar and season.

Mix the soft cheese with the remaining parsley and chives. Split and toast the muffins. Spread the soft cheese mixture over the muffin halves and place on serving plates. Top with the mushrooms and garnish with whole chives.

Vegetable Frittata

1 red capsicum (bell pepper), finely chopped
1 onion, finely chopped
1 zucchini (courgette), finely chopped
2¼ oz (70g) cabbage, finely chopped
1 head broccoli, cut into small florets
3 oz (90g) mushrooms, finely chopped
8 large eggs, beaten
4 oz (120g) aged Cheddar cheese, grated
½ cup parsley, chopped
Seasoned pepper
¹/₃ cup thickened cream

Preheat oven to 350°F (180°C) and lightly butter a large flan dish. Combine all ingredients and mix well, then pour into the dish.

Bake for 45–60 minutes until set – a skewer inserted in the middle should come out clean.

Granola Parfait

2 cups natural yoghurt
2 tbsps honey
½ tsp ground cinnamon
½ cup granola
2 tbsps walnuts or almonds, coarsely chopped
1½ cups chopped seasonal
Fruit such as blueberries, strawberries, kiwi fruit, peaches, mangoes, pears
2 sprigs mint

In a bowl, mix together yoghurt, honey and cinnamon.

Divide half of the yoghurt mixture between 4 parfait glasses. Add the granola, nuts and fruit. Cover with the remaining yoghurt mixture.

Separate the mint leaves and use as a garnish with a few extra fresh berries.

Fresh Fruit Smoothie

Serves 4

2 cups mixed fruit, for example, strawberries, blueberries, mango, papaya, apples
1 banana
¼ cup milk
⅓ cup orange juice

Place glasses into the freezer to pre-chill.

Remove any green tops from fruits such as strawberries. Peel the banana and place all fruit in a blender.

Top with milk, orange juice and half a cup of crushed ice. Blend for 2 minutes, or until all ingredients are combined.

Pour into chilled glasses, top with extra pieces of sliced fruit and serve immediately.

Sunrise Surprise Smoothie

Serves 4

2 blood oranges, peeled and deseeded
Pulp of 1 mango
Pulp of 4 passionfruit
1 cup natural yoghurt
2 tsps honey
4 drops vanilla extract

Place all ingredients in a blender with 8 ice cubes and blend until smooth. Pour into chilled glasses and serve topped with an extra dollop of yoghurt and some extra passionfruit pulp.

Mango Morning Smoothie

Serves 4

1 cup milk
1 mango
1 banana
1 cup natural yoghurt
4 tsps toasted muesli
2 tbsps date paste

Place all ingredients in a blender with 6 ice cubes and blend until smooth. Pour into chilled glasses and serve topped with an extra sprinkle of muesli.

Baked Eggs

Serves 2 • Preparation 10 minutes • Cooking 15 minutes

3½ oz (100g) spinach leaves, coarsely chopped
50g salted ricotta, sliced
¼ cup thickened cream
2 large eggs

Preheat the oven to 375°F (190°C).
Place two ramekins in a deep baking tray. Wash the spinach and cook in a medium saucepan over low heat until wilted. Drain off excess water. Transfer the spinach to a medium bowl. Add the ricotta and cream and stir to combine. Spoon the spinach mixture into the ramekins and break an egg into the centre.
Fill the baking tray with boiling water to come halfway up the sides of the ramekins. Bake in the oven for 15 minutes, or until the eggs have set.

Bacon and Avocado Muffin

Serves 2 • Preparation 5 minutes • Cooking 8 minutes

4 rashers bacon, halved and rind removed
2 English muffins, halved crosswise
2 tbsps mayonnaise
1 ripe avocado, halved and stone removed

Preheat a medium non-stick frying pan on medium-high heat. Cook the bacon for
2 minutes on each side or until crisp.
Toast the muffins in a toaster until golden brown. Spread mayonnaise on the muffin tops.
Slice the avocado and lay on the base of the muffins. Top with bacon slices and cover with muffin
tops.

Poached Eggs on Toast

Serves 2

4 large eggs
2 slices sourdough bread, about ¾ in (2cm) thick
⅓ cup beetroot chutney
1¾ oz (50g) rocket leaves

Bring a medium saucepan of water to the simmer. Using a spoon, create a whirlpool and crack the eggs one at a time into the centre. Poach for about 3 minutes or until whites are slightly firm.

Cook the bread in a toaster until golden brown. Arrange the toast, eggs, rocket and chutney onto two serving plates.

PREPARING YOUR PARTY
ETIQUETTE

MIND YOUR MANNERS

While the celebrations in this book are all about having fun and letting loose, it's important that manners are still observed in the planning stages and during your event, so you are not left to deal with an embarrassing situation or a guest who is upset or offended.

Send your RSVPs out as soon as possible to give people enough time to respond to your event. Try to ensure you have the date, time and location already locked in and give details about what to expect on the night. Be clear about the dress code, a matter of crucial importance to your guests. If you don't want anyone to wear jeans, or you have a specific theme in mind, make sure you specify the requirements. While not everyone will turn up on time, if you have transport, entertainment or a meal booked for a particular time ask guests to arrive 15 minutes early and politely request that they be punctual.

Someone will always ask if they can bring along extra guests. If you are catering for a certain head count, or your numbers are restricted by space or preference, make sure everyone knows that the event is invitation only to avoid any awkward situations. State this clearly on the invitation.

Don't forget, as a host it's your job to meet and greet your guests, and explain the schedule for the event. If they are bringing gifts, make sure you have a safe area in which to store them. When the party's over, it also falls to you to encourage possibly reluctant guests to move on. Sometimes people will overstay their welcome, so you may want to announce the exit time earlier in the event, or on the invitation. Make sure, of course, to thank everyone for coming.

Be careful not to drink too much, as it's not a good look to be the host who's had the most! Watch your alcohol intake until the party is almost over. Then you can relax with a glass of wine and be proud of your successful do.

Employing a little etiquette helps everyone, but especially the host, enjoy an effortlessly smooth and satisfying function.

NOTES

NOTES

NOTES

NOTES

NOTES

NOTES

A NOTE ON MEASUREMENTS

1 teaspoon = 5g/5ml
1 tablespoon = 15g/15ml
Liquid measures: 1 cup = 250ml (9fl oz)
Solid measures (vary, depending on substance): 1 cup caster sugar = 220g
(8 oz); 1 cup flour = 150g (5 oz); 1 cup white sugar = 225g (24 oz)

Published in 2013 by
New Holland Publishers
London • Sydney • Cape Town • Auckland

Garfield House 86–88 Edgware Road London W2 2EA United Kingdom
1/66 Gibbes Street Chatswood NSW 2067 Australia
Wembley Square First Floor Solan Road Gardens Cape Town 8001 South Africa
218 Lake Road Northcote Auckland New Zealand

Copyright © 2013 New Holland Publishers

www.newhollandpublishers.com

A catalogue record of this book is available at the British Library and the National Library of
Australia.

ISBN: 9781742573762

Publisher: Fiona Schultz
Design: Kim Pearce & Keisha Galbraith
Editor: Kate Sherington
Production Director: Olga Dementiev
Printer: Toppan Leefung Printing Ltd (China)

10 9 8 7 6 5 4 3 2 1

Follow New Holland Publishers on
Facebook: www.facebook.com/NewHollandPublishers